PROFILES

SIX BIOS

ADOLF HITLER

DWIGHT D. EISENHOWER

WINSTON CHURCHILL

WORLD WAR II

HIROHITO

JOSEF STALIN

FRANKLIN D. ROOSEVELT

BY AARON ROSENBERG

SCHOLASTIC INC.

New York   Toronto   London   Auckland
Sydney   Mexico City   New Delhi   Hong Kong

PHOTO CREDITS   *Photo Research: Dwayne Howard*

Cover: *Hitler:* DeAgostini/Getty Images; *Churchill:* Roger Viollet/Getty Images; *Stalin* & *Roosevelt:* Getty Images; *Hirohito:* AFP/Getty Images; *Eisenhower:* Time & Life Pictures/Getty Images.

Page 7: Granger Collection; page 8: Everett Collection Inc./Alamy; page 9 top: Pictorial Press Ltd./Alamy; page 9 bottom: Interfoto/Alamy; page 11: Adrian Sherratt/Alamy; pages 13–14: Granger Collection; page 16: Portrait of Karl Marx (1818–1893) (b/w photo), English Photographer, (19th century)/Private Collection/Bridgeman Art Library; pages 18, 21 top & bottom, 24: Granger Collection; page 26: Mary Evans Picture Library/Alamy; page 28: Associated Press; page 31: Keystone Pictures USA/Alamy; pages 32–33: Granger Collection; page 35 top: Getty Images; page 35 bottom: 1884 Keystone-France/Getty Images; pages 37–38, 41: Getty Images; page 43: Popperfoto/Getty Images; page 46: Granger Collection; pages 48–50: Associated Press; page 53: Getty Images; page 54: Everett Collection/SuperStock; pages 57 top & bottom, 58: Getty Images; page 60: Gamma-Keystone via Getty Images; page 61: Getty Images; page 62: Granger Collection; page 63: Getty Images; page 65: Hulton-Deutsch Collection/Corbis; pages 66, 68: Granger Collection; page 72: Popperfoto/Getty Images; pages 74, 76: Granger Collection; page 77: Vova Pomortzeff/Alamy; pages 79–80, 81 top & bottom, 82: Franklin D. Roosevelt Presidential Library and Museum; page 84: Acme Newspictures; page 90: Franklin D. Roosevelt Presidential Library and Museum; page 95: U.S. Navy photograph; page 96: Franklin D. Roosevelt Presidential Library and Museum; page 99: Library of Congress; page 102: Bettmann/Corbis; page 103: National Diet Library, Japan; page 104: Gamma-Keystone via Getty Images; page 105: Bettmann/Corbis; page 109: Associated Press; page 110: Getty Images; page 116: Associated Press; page 120: Bettmann/Corbis; page 121: Gamma-Keystone via Getty Images; page 123: Bettmann/Corbis; page 124: Wally NcNamee/Corbis; page 125: Associated Press; pages 127–128: Dwight D. Eisenhower Presidential Library and Museum; page 130: Dwight D. Eisenhower Presidential Library and Museum/AP; pages 131–132, 135: Dwight D. Eisenhower Presidential Library and Museum; page 136: Getty Images; pages 137–138: Associated Press; page 139: Granger Collection; page 143: National Park Service; page 148: John F. Kennedy Presidential Library and Museum; page 152: Scholastic Inc./Jim McMahon.

———

ISBN 978-0-545-31655-2

10 9 8 7 6 5 4 3 2 1   11 12 13 14 15

Printed in the U.S.A.   40
First edition, August 2011
Designed by Kay Petronio & Tim Hall

CONTENTS

INTRODUCTION

THE SECOND WORLD WAR, OR WORLD WAR II, BEGAN ON September 1, 1939, when Germany invaded Poland. Soon Germany, Italy, and Japan formed an **axis** of power. The United Kingdom, the United States, and the new **Soviet Union** eventually gathered to form the Allied forces, along with France and several other countries. The war lasted for six years, ending with Germany's surrender on May 7, 1945, and Japan's surrender on August 14. All told, the war cost roughly sixty million lives. It rewrote the face of the world and set the stage for world politics for years to come.

You can read plenty of books about the war itself, about specific battles, soldiers, and armies, or about what happened to certain countries during and after the war. But who were some of the major players behind this conflict? Who were the leaders of the Axis and the Allies? And how did their actions influence one another and the war?

Most people have heard of Adolf Hitler, but did you know he wanted to be a painter instead of a politician? Or that he served in the German army during World

War I? How did Josef Stalin become the undisputed ruler of the new Soviet Union, and why did he and Hitler form an alliance before World War II began if they disliked each other so much? Who was Hirohito, and how did he not only get Japan involved in the war but salvage the country after their defeat? Why did Winston Churchill warn against the new Soviet Union and then ally with it against Nazi Germany? Why did Franklin D. Roosevelt want the United States to join the war when the fighting was taking place so far away? How did Dwight D. Eisenhower become the supreme Allied commander when he never saw combat himself? And how did he help pick up the pieces after the war was over?

The six people in this book had a major effect on World War II and on one another. We'll see who these people were, what their lives were like, and where they intersected with one another. We'll find out how they influenced one another and the course of events, both during and after the war, and how they affected the entire world around them. Each of these people had a lasting influence. We are still feeling the effects of their actions, and their lives, today.

ADOLF HITLER

ADOLF HITLER was the undisputed ruler of Germany and the man who started World War II. He slaughtered millions of people in what became known as the Holocaust.

EARLY LIFE

ADOLF HITLER WAS BORN ON APRIL 20, 1889, in the town of Braunau am Inn. Braunau was in **Austria-Hungary** near the German border. His father, Alois, was an Austrian customs official. His mother, Klara, was Alois's third wife. Alois had two children from his second marriage. He and Klara had five other children besides Hitler. But three of those children died in infancy, and a fourth died before age six. Only Hitler and his little sister, Paula, survived.

Hitler did very well when he started school in 1895. He was bright and popular. Both teachers and students liked him. His father hoped this meant Hitler would continue to do well in school and then join the civil service like himself.

In 1897 the family moved from the farming town of Hafeld to the market town of Lambach. A year later they moved again, this time to the village of Leonding, on the outskirts of Linz. Hitler was forced to switch schools with each move. In 1900 he started secondary school and quickly ran into problems. There were more children in this school. Earning

Hitler as an infant

Hitler
at age 10

top grades was harder. Making friends was also harder. Hitler wasn't used to struggling at school, so he simply stopped trying. That upset his father and caused trouble between them. Hitler and his father struggled to get along.

Hitler's little brother, Edmund, had died that same year, in February 1900. Edmund's death upset Hitler a great deal.

There were two subjects Hitler liked. The first was history. His history teacher, Leopold Pötsch, was a German **Nationalist**. Pötsch taught Hitler and the other students that Germany was the greatest country in the world, and that the other nations were jealous and kept holding it back. That included Austria-Hungary. Most people along the border considered themselves both Austrians and Germans, but Hitler wanted nothing to do with Austria-Hungary. Part of that was his anger toward his strict, disapproving father. Alois was fiercely loyal to Austria-Hungary, which only made Hitler hate his birth country more.

Hitler's favorite subject, however, was art. He decided

to become an artist when he finished school. Alois was furious. He thought art was a waste of time and a waste of Hitler's talents. The two fought about Hitler's choice for several years. Hitler had actually wanted to go to a regular high school so he could start studying art more easily, but his father sent him to a technical high school instead.

Hitler's mother, Klara Polzl

Alois died when Hitler was only thirteen years old. The government gave their family a pension, or retirement fund, because Alois had been in the civil service. Hitler, his sister, and his mother were able to live comfortably on the money they received.

Hitler's mother had always spoiled him, but now that his father was gone, Hitler was allowed to do what he wanted. He enrolled in a regular high school in 1904, but by then he had gotten

Hitler's father, Alois

into the habit of goofing off rather than studying. Soon he stopped studying at all. His grades plummeted. When he was fifteen Hitler did so poorly on the school exams that his teachers said he would have to repeat the year. Instead he quit school completely.

DAYS IN VIENNA

Now that he was done with school, Hitler was free to choose his own path. He decided to move to Vienna and pursue his dream of being an artist. Vienna was the cultural center of Austria-Hungary. It had a reputation for art, music, and culture. Hitler was so attracted to the art in Vienna, he moved there even though it was part of Austria-Hungary.

Hitler applied to the Academy of Fine Arts in Vienna, but they rejected him. He was devastated. He had always thought he was good at art, and had never expected to fail.

The Rector did suggest that Hitler's talents lay in architecture, but he could not bring himself to apply to a second school. Plus he probably knew they would never accept a student who had not completed secondary school.

Hitler decided not to go back to Linz. He didn't want to admit to his mother that the Academy had turned him down. Instead he stayed in Vienna and pretended to be an art student. He spent his time reading, studying buildings, going to museums, taking long walks, and doing sketches.

He had just enough money to survive without needing a real job.

His mother, Klara, died in 1907. Hitler was crushed. He had adored his mother. Now he had no reason to return to Linz, which he had always considered his hometown. But he also had no money. He had given his sister, Paula, the rest of

Painting thought to have been done by Hitler

their father's benefits because she needed the money. Hitler survived by painting, but only barely. He copied images from postcards and sold the paintings to tourists. He applied to the Academy of Fine Arts again, but they rejected him a second time. His paintings were not selling well. In 1909 Hitler wound up living in a homeless shelter. In 1910 he settled into a house for poor working men. Around the same time Hitler started claiming that he was an anti-Semite, or someone who hated Jews. Vienna had a large Jewish community. Many of the Jews there were wealthy merchants who had fled attacks in Russia and taken refuge in the city. Many politicians and leaders had begun to rant about Jews and others who did not look or act like traditional Austrians.

GOING TO WAR

Every young man in Austria-Hungary was required to sign up for military service when he turned eighteen. But Hitler had no interest in serving in the military, or of serving Austria-Hungary in any way. So when Hitler received his call-up papers in 1909, he ignored them.

It took the government officials four years to find Hitler. They were looking for him in Linz and then in Vienna, but in 1913 Hitler had moved to Munich, Germany, instead. With the help of the Munich police, the Austro-Hungarian government caught up with Hitler. He was forced to take the entrance tests for the Austro-Hungarian army. He was both relieved and embarrassed when he didn't pass the physical. The doctors wrote that he was "unfit for combatant and auxiliary duty—too weak. Unable to bear arms."

In the summer of 1914, however, a war broke out. It was a war like no other. Many called it the Great War, or the War to End All Wars (later called World War I). Germany and Austria-Hungary were right in the middle of it.

The Great War was sparked on June 28, 1914, when an assassin killed Archduke Franz Ferdinand of Austria. He was the heir to the throne of Austria-Hungary. The assassin was from Serbia. Ferdinand's death prompted Austria-Hungary to finally declare war on Serbia on July 28. Russia supported Serbia. The German Empire supported Austria-Hungary. France used the new conflict as an excuse to attack Germany. Britain and Italy also got involved, more to protect their allies than to gain control over more land themselves. Italy actually had a Triple Alliance with Germany and Austria-Hungary at the time, but chose to side with France, Britain, and Russia instead.

Because Germany was at war and needed as many soldiers as it could get, it relaxed its army's entrance requirements. Hitler was allowed to sign up for service. Although he had avoided the original call to service, Hitler was now eager to participate. He even said, "I was overcome with impetuous enthusiasm, and falling on my knees, wholeheartedly thanked Heaven that I had been granted the happiness to live at this time." But Hitler didn't join the Austro-Hungarian army. He went to fight for Germany instead.

Hitler was soon given the job of dispatch runner. There were no telegraphs or telephones on the field then, so the only way to get a message to someone in the middle of a battle was to write a note and send someone to hand the note to him! The job was incredibly

Hitler in 1914, while serving in the German army

dangerous because the runners were constantly on the front line, where the soldiers were actively fighting. Dispatch runners also relied on speed, so they didn't have much in the way of protection or weapons.

Hitler loved his job. And he proved very good at it. He won five medals during the war, including the Iron Cross. His commanding officer wrote that "as a dispatch runner, he has shown cold-blooded courage and exemplary boldness. Under conditions of great peril, when all the communication lines were cut, the untiring and fearless activity of Hitler made it possible for important messages to go through." Hitler was promoted to the rank of corporal. He never got another promotion, however. Despite his courage, many of

Hitler (far right) with other wounded German soldiers during World War I

Hitler's fellow soldiers thought he was strange because he spent most of his time just sitting silently, waiting for an order. Hitler had requested not to be considered for further promotions because he didn't want to be transferred.

In October 1918 the British lobbed **mustard gas** at the German troops during an attack. The acrid smoke blinded Hitler. He was taken to a military hospital and kept there while he recovered. Fortunately the damage to his eyes was not permanent. But while he was still in the hospital the war ended. Austria-Hungary had fallen apart completely. The Russian Empire had become the a collection of Soviet republics. Germany surrendered and signed a cease-fire on November 11, 1918. The following year, on June 28, Germany and the other nations signed the Treaty of Versailles. In the treaty, Germany took full responsibility for starting the war. That meant they had to disarm their soldiers, disband most of their army, and pay the other affected countries for the damage the war had caused. The total cost was one hundred and thirty-two billion German marks. That would be equivalent to about four hundred billion dollars today!

When Hitler learned that Germany had surrendered, he became horribly depressed. He had believed in the cause and spent four years fighting, and for nothing. Another of his endeavors had ended in failure.

"THE NEW MESSIAH"

After the war Hitler returned to Munich, in Bavaria, a state of Germany. On November 7, 1918, Kurt Eisner, the leader of the Independent Democratic Socialist Party, declared Bavaria a **Socialist republic**. Socialism is a political belief that workers should be the ones in power. No one has authority over anyone else, and everyone works together. Karl Marx created the theory of Socialism.

Karl Marx

Hitler was horrified. He hated the idea of Socialism. He did not think all people were equal—some were born to lead and some were born to follow. A few months later, in May 1919, the German army swept into Munich and crushed the Republic. They arrested all the soldiers there and tried them as Socialists and traitors. Hitler managed to avoid being discharged or arrested, however. He even served on a three-person committee to identify those soldiers who had supported the Republic. In June the army transferred Hitler to the military intelligence unit investigating activities in Munich.

Germany was beginning to experience difficulties now

that the war was over. They had lost a great deal of money, land, and power after their surrender. Jobs were becoming scarce and money was tight for most people. Everyone was upset and looking for someone to blame.

In July 1919 Hitler was given a new assignment. He was ordered to infiltrate the German Workers' Party, or DAP. The DAP was a new political group, small but very active. The German officials wanted to know the DAP's real goals. Hitler went to several DAP meetings and listened to one of the group's founders, Anton Drexler, speak. Drexler believed in a strong, active German government. He blamed Jews, foreigners, Marxists, and capitalists (whom he considered people out only to make money for themselves) for Germany's problems.

Hitler agreed with Drexler. He met with the man and impressed Drexler with his own speaking skills. Drexler invited Hitler to join the DAP. Hitler accepted on September 12, 1919. He was the DAP's fifty-fifth member. He was soon invited to join the executive committee as well. The party changed its name to the National Socialist German Workers' Party, or NSDAP. "National Socialist" soon became shortened to the group's new nickname, the Nazi Party.

In March 1920 Hitler finished his military service and was discharged from the German army. His former

Hitler in Nazi
uniform

commanding officers encouraged him to continue with the Nazi Party. He perfected his skill at public speaking. Then he began talking to large crowds. Hitler complained about the Treaty of Versailles. He spoke about how unfairly the other nations had treated Germany after the war. He blamed its defeat on the politicians who had been in power then. He said those politicians had betrayed the army. They had surrendered the war even though the army had been undefeated in battle. According to Hitler, these traitors were mostly Marxists, capitalists, and Jews.

More and more people began listening to the Nazi Party's statements. Thousands came to listen to Hitler's speeches and wore the party's swastika emblem. The swastika was an ancient symbol that meant good luck and success. It was now also seen as a symbol of a Nordic master race. The Nordics are tall, blond people from northern Europe. Germany is considered a Nordic country. Hitler supported this idea. He wanted to identify the Nazis with the Nordic race instead of with groups he considered weaker, like Jews,

Gypsies (Eastern European wanderers who Hitler thought caused trouble in the towns they visited), and Marxists. He used the swastika to represent the Nordic connection.

In July 1921 Hitler went to Berlin to visit nationalist groups there. While he was gone, the Nazi Party's executive committee formed an alliance with a group of Socialists. When Hitler heard of this, he rushed back to Munich and threatened to resign from the party at once. The other committee members knew he had become too important for them to lose. Hitler knew that, too. He demanded control over the party. He forced them to put the question to a general vote, and won easily. On July 29, 1921, Hitler was introduced to the Nazi party as their führer, or leader.

MEIN KAMPF

In 1923 Hitler decided to take control of more than just the Nazi Party. The Italian politician Benito Mussolini had staged a march on Rome in late October 1922, marching almost thirty thousand men through the streets of Rome to demonstrate that he was prepared to use force to take control of Italy. The Italian king, Victor Emmanuel III, was afraid of a civil war. He handed control of the country over to Mussolini on October 29. Hitler hoped for a similar and equally easy outcome in Munich. He gathered his Nazis, particularly his private soldiers, the *Sturmabteilung*, or "Storm Section."

Bavaria's commissioner, Gustav von Kahr, was speaking to a large crowd at a beer hall on November 8. Hitler marched in and took control. He captured not only von Kahr but also the two other men who ruled Bavaria together, Colonel Hans Ritter von Seisser and General Otto von Lossow. Hitler ordered them to turn control over to him if they wanted to live. After arguing and resisting for hours, the three men finally agreed.

The next day, Hitler and his followers left the beer hall to march on the Bavarian Defense Ministry. But they encountered a squad of one hundred soldiers along the way. Shots were exchanged and many of the Nazis simply fled. Hitler was arrested two days later and charged with **treason**. His trial began on February 26, 1924. He was sentenced to five years in prison in Landsberg Castle, one of the nicer prisons with no hard labor and with comfortable cells.

Surprisingly, Hitler did not mind going to prison. His speech during the trial had made him a national celebrity, so he was treated well. He used his time in prison to read a great deal of German history and political philosophy. He even described his prison time as a "free education at the state's expense." He read American carmaker Henry Ford's autobiography, *My Life and Work*, and Ford's book *The*

International Jew. Hitler decided to write his own autobiography, although he preferred to dictate it rather than write it himself. His friend Rudolf Hess assisted him. Hitler originally called the book *Four Years of Struggle against Lies, Stupidity,*

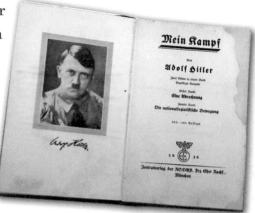

and Cowardice, but his publisher shortened that to just *My Struggle,* or, in German, *Mein Kampf.*

Hitler was released from prison on December 20, 1924. He continued to work on his book once he was a free man. He didn't bother with historical accuracy in *Mein Kampf.* He changed or downplayed details of his life to put himself in a better light. The book also served to explain his philosophy, however. The first volume was published in 1925 and the second in 1927. The books had sold more than two hundred and forty thousand copies by 1934.

Hitler after he was released from prison in 1924

HOW HITLER FELT ABOUT HIS AUDIENCE

Hitler's greatest gift was his ability to sway people with his speeches. His secret was to treat them like children. As he wrote in *Mein Kampf*:

"The masses find it difficult to understand politics, their intelligence is small. Therefore all effective **propaganda** must be limited to a very few points. The masses will only remember only the simplest ideas repeated a thousand times over. If I approach the masses with reasoned arguments, they will not understand me. In the mass meeting, their reasoning power is paralyzed. What I say is like an order given under hypnosis."

DAS FÜHRER

Hitler resumed control of the Nazi Party after his release. By then they had over nine hundred thousand members. But that didn't mean much in politics. The important thing was the number of seats a party could win in Germany's parliament. With enough seats a party could control votes, which gave them effective control of the country. And for all its members, the Nazis had only fourteen seats in December 1924. That was only 3 percent of the parliament.

That all changed, however, after the New York stock market crashed in 1929. The New York stock market both reflected and, to some degree, controlled the value of various goods in the United States. Stocks represented those goods, and shares in the companies that produced them. People bought, sold, and traded the stocks to make money. But the United States had let prices get too high and nobody had money to buy anything anymore. The stock market crashed as a result, and a period called the Great Depression followed. The sudden collapse affected economies around the world, including Germany's. The United States started demanding more of the money Germany had agreed to pay them. By September 1930 Germany was facing a Great Depression of its own. Everyone was worried and scared and looking for answers. They also wanted someone to blame. By September 1930 the Nazi party had over six million votes and 107 seats. By July 1932 the number had doubled, with almost fourteen million votes and over 230 seats. That gave the Nazi party a little less than 38 percent of the vote. Hitler was running for president of Germany at the time. He came in second to the existing president, Paul von Hindenburg.

After the election, Hitler had the sudden realization that he couldn't legally run for office. He wasn't a German citizen! He had renounced his Austrian citizenship in 1925 but had never yet applied for German citizenship. One of the Nazis was an interior minister of Brunswick, however. He appointed Hitler as administrator for the state's delegation to the military in Berlin. That automatically made Hitler

Hitler with Hindenburg in 1933

a citizen of Brunswick. Because Brunswick was a German city, he was now officially a German citizen.

Several influential businessmen took interest in the Nazis after the failed election. They contributed money to the party. They also put pressure on Hindenburg to make Hitler a government leader. The president finally agreed to create a new **coalition** government consisting of the Nazi Party and his own German National People's Party, or DNVP. Hitler was appointed chancellor of Germany on January 30, 1933. Two other Nazis were given major positions. Wilhelm Frick became minister of the interior. Hermann Göring became minister without portfolio, which meant he was a minister with no specified duties. Another

Nazi was made vice-chancellor and a fourth became minister of the economy.

Because no one party had a majority in the Reichstag, or parliament, Hitler persuaded Hindenburg to dissolve it in early 1933. New votes were taken and the Nazis now held almost 44 percent, but still not a clear majority. To make up for that, in late March Hitler proposed an Enabling Act that would give the **cabinet** the power to make laws without the Reichstag's approval for the next four years. A two-thirds majority approved the act. Now Hitler and his two ministers essentially controlled the entire government. He dissolved both the Communist Party and the Social Democratic Party. Next Hitler crushed the trade unions (organizations of people with the same skills who worked the same jobs) and forced the workers to swear allegiance to him. The government was dissolved and absorbed into smaller political groups. By July 14 he had declared the Nazi Party the only legal party in Germany.

President Paul von Hindenburg died on August 2, 1934. Hitler passed a law transferring the role and powers of the presidency to himself as *führer und reichskanzler*, leader and chancellor. He was now the supreme ruler of Germany.

THE THIRD REICH

Hitler was not satisfied with Germany's current status,

however. He wanted the return to glory he had promised all those who had listened to his speeches. He increased the size of the army, ignoring the rules of the Treaty of Versailles. He attempted to form an alliance with Britain, but Britain refused. Hitler did speak to neighboring Poland. They formed the German-Polish Nonaggression **Pact** of January 1934. This was the first of Nazi Germany's new alliances.

In March 1935 Hitler publicly rejected the Treaty of Versailles and announced that he was expanding the German army, increasing the size of the navy, and restoring the air force. Britain, Italy, France, and the League of Nations all protested, but no one made any moves to stop him. In June he signed an Anglo-German Naval Agreement with Britain, allowing him to increase the German navy as long as it stayed smaller than 35 percent of the British navy

Hitler in Nuremberg, 1935

(and had roughly half the British navy's number of submarines). Back at home, however, the Nazi party had already
begun acts of assault and violence against German Jews.
On September 15 Hitler passed laws banning sex and marriage between Jews and "Aryans," as he called true Nordic
Germans, and assigning Jews to a lower class of citizenship.
The German government also prohibited Aryan women
under age forty-five from working in Jewish households.

Hitler was working to establish ties with nations he
thought could help Germany achieve greater power. On
October 25, 1936, Germany and Italy declared an axis,
or alliance. A month later Germany signed a pact with
Japan. Two years later, in February 1938, Hitler withdrew
German support of China, ending the unofficial alliance
between those two nations and strengthening Germany's
bond with Japan. A month later he pressured Austria into
uniting with Germany. Austria was too weak to resist.

In late September 1938 the Munich Agreement between
Hitler; Mussolini; Britain's prime minister, Neville
Chamberlain; and France's prime minister, Édouard
Daladier, gave the Sudetenland (western regions of
Czechoslovakia) back to Germany. Britain and France
were most concerned about the possibility of an alli-
ance between Germany and the Soviet Union. They felt
that giving Germany the Sudetenland was a small price

to pay if it prevented an alliance between the two countries. But in March of 1939 Germany seized the rest of Czechoslovakia anyway, breaking the Munich Agreement. Then on September 1, 1939, Germany invaded western Poland. Britain and France declared war on Germany two days later, but didn't take any direct action. Hitler invaded eastern Poland two weeks later, on the 17th. Now Germany held all of Poland.

Hitler had accused the Marxists of helping ruin Germany. He considered Josef Stalin, the Soviet president, the worst kind of man. But Hitler had to put personal feelings aside in favor of reason and strategy. The new Soviet Union was one of the world's superpowers. Hitler had no desire to go up against a country with such a large military. In 1939 Germany surprised everyone when it formed a nonaggression pact, the Nazi-Soviet Pact, with the Soviet Union.

Hitler inspecting his troops in Poland

In April 1940 Germany invaded Denmark and Norway. Hitler invaded France in May, and took control of Luxembourg, the Netherlands, and Belgium along the way. Italy's soldiers joined the German soldiers on June 10. France surrendered on June 22.

Then, in 1941, Hitler made a fatal mistake. He ignored his pact with Stalin and sent the German army into the Soviet Union. Hitler hoped to crush any resistance and take control of the major Soviet cities quickly. He had not counted on the sheer size of the Soviet Union. He had also underestimated its most powerful defense—the deadly Soviet winter. The German army had to turn back from its attempts to reach Moscow in December of that year and from its attempts to invade Stalingrad over the next two winters as well.

The United States had deliberately stayed out of the European conflict. The American president, Franklin Delano Roosevelt, had no desire to fight a long and costly war that did not concern the United States directly. He sent aid to France and Britain but no troops. That changed in December 1941 when Japan attacked American troops at Pearl Harbor. The United States joined the Alliance of European countries battling Germany, Italy, and Japan. U.S. soldiers poured in to reinforce the British and French troops. Hitler's army was tired from two years of battle.

Now they were facing fresh, young soldiers. The war was turning against Hitler.

Over the next few years Germany lost its early advantage. Its strongest supporter, Italy, fell to the Allies on September 8, 1943. The Allies reclaimed France from German troops in August 1944. Then they pushed Hitler's forces back into Germany itself. By early 1945 it became clear that this war, which had become even larger and more deadly than World War I, would soon be over.

THE HOLOCAUST

Hitler did not spend all of his time and energy attacking other nations. He was also battling Jews, Marxists, Gypsies, homosexuals, and other people whom he saw as the "undesirables" who had "weakened" Germany for so long. In 1941 he had begun what he called his Final Solution. The solution was horrifying: Hitler's forces rounded up the people who belonged to the "problem" groups and held them in concentration camps all over Europe until they could be killed. At first Hitler's guards shot them. When shooting proved too time-consuming and expensive, he ordered them to be gassed, or poisoned, in enormous mass showers. Thousands upon thousands of bodies were dumped into mass graves. Every country Hitler invaded had to turn over their undesirables. Long trains carried Jews and the others on Hitler's list to camps to await their death.

Historians later gave this sad and gruesome period a name: the Holocaust. The word means "wholesale destruction" or "calamity." Over six million Jews were killed in the course of a dozen years, and over eleven million people in all. Hitler had set out to completely exterminate the Jewish people. He succeeded in killing two-thirds of the existing Jewish population of Europe.

When the Allies took control of Germany and its territories, the soldiers discovered the concentration camps. They were appalled. People had been treated worse than animals. Heads had been shaved so that the camp guards could sell the hair. Gold teeth had been wrenched out and sold. Numbers had been tattooed onto the insides of wrists for identification purposes. Men and women were kept completely separate. Sometimes a husband and wife would live in the same camp for years but never even know the other was still alive. Children were either left with their mothers or

Boy holding his hands up during the Holocaust

separated from both parents until they became old enough to go into either the men's camps or the women's camps. Those who had survived were quickly freed. No one could believe the terrible things that the Nazis had done to these prisoners. Hitler quickly went from being seen as a harsh dictator to a true monster.

THE END

Hitler's attack on the Soviet Union freed Stalin to join the Allies. In January 1945 Stalin's forces crashed into Germany's eastern border. The German forces could not stand against them. Hitler had already fled his headquarters in East Prussia. He was now hiding in a bunker in Berlin. Everyone knew the end was near.

Hitler's health had collapsed over the last few years. Every failure in the war seemed to crush him personally.

The ruins of Hitler's bunker

He looked old and feeble even though he was only sixty-five. But Hitler was determined not to become a prisoner. He knew the Soviets would deliberately humiliate him if he were caught. And he knew the other nations would put him on trial for war crimes. Hitler could not live with the idea of being paraded through the streets or held up to ridicule.

On April 28, Hitler married Eva Braun, whom he had a long-term relationship with. He had always refused to consider marriage before.

On April 30, the two of them went into a private room in the bunker. They both took poison tablets, and Hitler shot himself in the head. Once they were both dead, the few loyal soldiers left in the bunker carried the bodies outside. They burned the remains so no one could find them and put them on display. The lack of a body created an air of mystery around Hitler's death. For many years people wondered if he had faked his death and escaped completely.

Hitler with Eva Braun

Hitler wanted to see Germany grow strong again. But he became obsessed with conquering the world and removing those he considered undesirable. Hitler was a powerful leader, but his twisted vision drove the whole world to war and almost killed an entire group of people.

WINSTON CHURCHILL

SIR WINSTON CHURCHILL was prime minister of Great Britain during World War II. His strong leadership helped guide his nation and the world through the difficult war years.

EARLY LIFE

Winston Leonard Spencer Churchill was born on November 30, 1874, at the Duke of Marlborough's palace in Woodstock, Oxfordshire, England. His father, Lord Randolph Churchill, was the third and youngest son of the seventh Duke of Marlborough and a politician. His mother, who had been born Jennie Jerome but was now known as Lady Randolph Churchill, was the daughter of an American millionaire. Churchill had an older brother named John Strange Spencer Churchill.

Churchill's father, Lord Randolph Churchill

The Churchills were busy, important people. Lord Randolph was often away at **Parliament**, and Lady Randolph attended many social events and participated in charities. They were not very attentive parents. But they

Churchill at age 10; his mother, Jennie Jerome; and his brother, Jack

made sure their two sons were looked after properly. Lady Randolph hired a nanny named Elizabeth Everest to take care of young Churchill and his brother.

EDUCATION

At first Churchill's nanny brought a governess in to educate him at home. But in 1882 he was sent to St. George's School in Ascot, Berkshire. He was seven years old. It was a typical boarding school. That meant Churchill lived there. He later wrote, "It appears that I was to go away from home for many weeks at a stretch in order to do lessons under masters. . . . After all I was only seven, and I had been so happy in my nursery with all my toys. I had such wonderful toys: a real steam engine, a magic lantern, and a collection of soldiers already nearly a thousand strong. Now it was to be all lessons."

Churchill did not do well at St. George's. He was a proud and independent little boy who had never left home before. Now he was forced to take lessons in subjects that did not interest him. He was also, from the start, determined to have his own way in things.

In 1884 Churchill was transferred to the Misses Thomsons' preparatory school in Hove, near Brighton. He was happier there than he had been at St. George's, in part because he found subjects that appealed to him. He was particularly fond of French, history, poetry, horseback riding, and swimming.

Churchill as a Harrow schoolboy

In 1888 Churchill changed schools again. This time he moved to Harrow School, a boy's school near London. Harrow was not an easy school, and Churchill had trouble with some of his studies. "I was on the whole considerably discouraged by my school days," he later wrote. However, he got excellent grades in both English and history, and became the school's fencing champion. Churchill also joined the Harrow Rifle Corps and learned to shoot. Harrow, like many schools at that time, prepared its students for the possibility of a career in the military.

Churchill did not see his parents much during this time. They rarely visited him in school, and he hardly ever went home for the various holidays. Lord Randolph died in January 1895, at forty-five. Churchill had never been close with his father, but regretted never getting to know him.

He also became convinced that his father's death meant he, too, would die at a young age. Churchill decided then and there to make sure he lived a full life during whatever time he had left.

MILITARY CORRESPONDENCE

As his schooling drew to a close, Churchill applied to the Royal Military College in Sandhurst. He failed the entry exams, but Churchill was not one to quit. He tried again, and failed a second time. He tried a third time after graduating from Harrow in 1892, and this time he passed. He had selected the cavalry (mounted troops) rather than the

Churchill at Sandhurst

infantry (foot soldiers), both because he loved horseback riding and because the cavalry did not require him to learn any more math. Churchill graduated from the academy in December 1894, eighth in his class out of one hundred and fifty students. He was offered the chance to transfer to infantry but decided to stay with the cavalry instead. He received a commission of second lieutenant in the Fourth Hussars on February 20, 1895. Churchill was now a military man.

That same year, Churchill received his first assignment. He was sent to Cuba to observe the battle between Spanish forces and Cuban **guerillas**. The assignment was not from his commanding officers, however. The *Daily Graphic* newspaper had offered Churchill a commission to write about the conflict. He enjoyed his time in Cuba and said the island was rich and beautiful. On the way there and on the way home Churchill stopped in New York and stayed for a while with Bourke Cockran, a friend of his mother's. Cockran was a member of the United States House of Representatives. Churchill gained a great deal from watching his new friend's techniques for handling conversation and politics.

In 1896 Churchill traveled to India, and in 1897 he fought along the North-West Frontier. During that time he experienced a two-week battle between the British forces and India's native tribes. Churchill's account of the battle named the Siege of Malakand was published in 1898 as the book *The Story of the Malakand Field Force*. The publication led to more articles for newspapers like the *Morning Post*. In 1898 Churchill went to the Sudan, then ruled by

Britain and Egypt, as a soldier. That September he participated in the last major British cavalry charge at the Battle of Omdurman. New inventions like the motorcycle were replacing horses in battle. In October he returned to Britain and began writing *The River War*, a two-volume account of the reconquest of the Sudan. Churchill resigned from the British army the following year, as of May 5, 1899.

Churchill first entered politics right after leaving the army. Robert Ascroft, a respected British politician at the time, invited him to become the second Conservative Party candidate in Oldham for the British parliament. But Ascroft died suddenly, and Churchill was unable to win a seat without the veteran politician's support. Instead he obtained a commission to serve as a **war correspondent** for the *Morning Post* and was sent to Africa to cover the Second Boer War between Britain and the small South African countries known as the Boer republics. The war began on October 11, and Churchill set sail for Africa a few days later.

Unfortunately, Churchill was with an armored train on a scouting expedition in November when Boer soldiers captured it. Churchill and the soldiers were taken prisoner and sent to a prison in Pretoria, thirty-four miles north of Johannesburg. The prison was called the State Model

Schools. It had been a teachers' college before the soldiers had converted it.

Churchill remained a captive for almost a month. He refused to give up hope, however, and constantly watched for an opportunity to escape. He even planned an escape with two other prisoners, but they never acted on that plan. On December 12 he found his chance. The guards had turned their backs for a moment, and Churchill seized the opportunity. He quickly climbed the wall to the other side. Luckily, he was not a soldier so he was not wearing a uniform. In his brown flannel suit, Churchill was able to blend in with the residents of Pretoria. He waited until he found a departing train. Then he jumped into an open train car and hid among sacks of coal dust.

The next day Churchill left the train and knocked on a random door. Fortunately, the home belonged to a fellow Englishman, a Mr. John Howard. Howard was a mine manager, and hid Churchill in a coal mine before helping him squeeze into a train car loaded with bales of wool. The train

Churchill in Durban after escaping from Pretoria

carried Churchill safely to Delagoa Bay in southeastern Africa. From there he went on to Durban and rejoined the British army. His daring escape earned Churchill the reputation of a hero. When the British troops marched to Pretoria, Churchill returned with them. He went straight to his former prison, demanded the surrender of the prison guards, and freed the soldiers who were being held.

POLITICAL GAMES

In 1900 Churchill returned to England. He campaigned for a seat in Parliament in Oldham again, and this time he won. He was now renowned as both a war hero and a war correspondent. He went on a speaking tour of Britain, followed by speaking tours of the United States and Canada. His talks drew large crowds and a great deal of admiration.

Churchill was elected as a member of the Conservative party. He spoke out against military spending and extra taxes. However, the Conservatives backed both plans, and Churchill's stance alienated him from his own party. In 1904 he became a member of the Liberal Party instead. The following year, Henry Campbell-Bannerman became prime minister. Campbell-Bannerman was also a Liberal. He appointed Churchill as undersecretary of state for the colonies, which mainly meant South Africa.

This was a very important year for Churchill. He attended a ball at Crewe House, in honor of the Earl of Crewe, and met a young woman named Clementine Hozier. They met again in 1908 at a dinner party. Churchill was smitten with Hozier. He proposed to her on August 11, 1908. They were married a month later, on September 12, in Westminster. The young couple moved into a house in London the following year, and their first child, Diana, was born on July 11, 1909. They had four more children: Randolph in 1911, Sarah in 1914, Marigold in 1918, and Mary in 1922. Sadly, Marigold died in 1921, but the others all lived to adulthood.

Churchill worked hard at his appointment, and in 1910 he was promoted to home secretary. He was transferred to the office of the first lord of the admiralty in 1911. There he helped develop naval aviation, construct new warships and tanks, and switch the Royal Navy from using coal to using oil for fuel.

Churchill and his wife, Clementine Hozier

In 1915, after World War I had begun, Churchill supported a major plan to secure a sea route to Russia. His rivals forced him to take full responsibility when the attempt failed and resign his post from the Royal Navy on November 15. He then joined the British army as a lieutenant colonel and commanded the Sixth Battalion of the Royal Scots Fusiliers. His bravery impressed his soldiers. In June 1916 Churchill returned to government service and became a private member of Parliament. In July 1917 he became minister of munitions. Less than two years later he was appointed secretary of state for war and air.

One of Churchill's greatest concerns during this time was the Russian Civil War. He believed that Communism was dangerous and urged Britain to intervene. Communism is a form of Socialism with the belief that everyone should be a part of the working community and the government operates under a one-party system. After British troops withdrew in 1920, Churchill made sure they sent weapons to the Poles who were invading the Ukraine in order to keep the pressure on the newly established collection of socialist republics.

In 1921 he became secretary of state for the colonies. He helped draft the Anglo-Irish Treaty of 1921, which created the Irish Free State. He made sure, however, that Britain still had use of three major Irish ports for its navy.

In 1923 Churchill ran for prime minister as a Liberal, and lost. He left the Liberal Party after that because he didn't have faith that the party could be organized enough to make a difference. He ran again, as an Independent and then as a Constitutionalist. He became chancellor of the exchequer in 1924. That meant that he was now in charge of the treasury. But he made several bad decisions in that post. The first was in 1925 to return to a gold standard (in which all money is based upon the current value of gold). That led to unemployment and deflation as prices dropped too quickly. The second was his mishandling of the nation's budget.

Even though his job was with the treasury, Churchill still kept a watchful eye on world events. He saw that Germany was getting poorer and more desperate, which made it a dangerous country. Churchill urged Britain to crack down on Germany and make sure it did not violate the Treaty of Versailles. His superiors ignored his warning, however.

Churchill had angered many people over the years while holding his various political positions. As a result, he was unable to gain any political office from 1929 to 1939. He dubbed that period "the wilderness years" and concentrated instead on his writing. He continued to speak about politics. He spoke most often about the increasing danger of Germany's rising aggression. On September 3, 1939, Britain declared war on Germany. That same day, Prime Minister Chamberlain offered Churchill his old post as first lord of the admiralty, and the associated position on the war cabinet. Churchill accepted.

One of Churchill's first suggestions was to occupy Norway and Sweden to keep them from falling to Germany. Chamberlain disagreed, however. The British troops stayed put, and Germany invaded Norway unopposed. As a result, the British people lost confidence in Chamberlain's ability to lead during the war. He resigned, and King George VI officially offered Churchill the post. In May 1940 Churchill became the new prime minister.

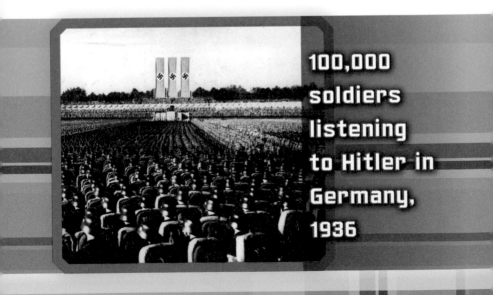

100,000 soldiers listening to Hitler in Germany, 1936

WILLING TO DEAL

Despite speaking frequently against Communism and the new Soviet Union, on May 4, 1939, Churchill spoke about the Soviet Union's recent offer to ally with Great Britain and France. He supported the idea. Churchill said:

"There is no means of maintaining an eastern front against Nazi aggression without the active aid of Russia. Russian interests are deeply concerned in preventing Herr Hitler's designs on Eastern Europe. It should still be possible to range all the States and peoples from the Baltic to the Black Sea in one solid front against a new outrage or invasion. Such a front, if established in good heart, and with resolute and efficient military arrangements, combined with the strength of the Western Powers, may yet confront Hitler . . . with forces the German people would be reluctant to challenge."

GUIDING THE WAR

There were still British citizens who hoped to find a peaceful solution for the current conflict. But Churchill knew better. The time for peace had passed. This was a time for war. On June 18, 1940, he told the **House of Commons**, "I expect that the Battle of Britain is about to begin."

Churchill's powerful speeches convinced the British that they could not expect a quick or easy resolution to this war. He also refused to consider any of the alliances and pacts Germany offered. Churchill knew there was no reasoning with a man like Hitler. Any agreement would only last until Hitler decided to break it, and Britain would look weak for bargaining in the first place. Instead he focused the country on defending itself and on preparing to take the fight to Germany. As he told the British people, "we shall fight in France, we shall fight on the seas and oceans, we shall fight with growing confidence and growing strength in the air, we shall defend our island, whatever the cost may be, we shall fight on the beaches, we shall fight on the landing grounds, we shall fight in the fields and in the streets, we shall fight in the hills; we shall never surrender."

Royal Air Force balloon flying over London in 1940

One of Churchill's greatest triumphs during the war was maintaining good relations with the United States. He had struck up a friendship with American President Franklin D. Roosevelt, and used the bond between the two countries to get food, oil, and weapons for British troops. Churchill and

Crowded London subway tunnel during heavy bombing

Roosevelt had twelve strategic conferences during the course of the war. Churchill even addressed the U.S. Congress on December 26, 1941. He was also friends with Harry S. Truman, who succeeded Roosevelt in office near the end of the war. Churchill helped support Truman during those difficult first days.

Churchill had done his best to defeat the Bolsheviks during the Russian Civil War. When that failed he had tried to at least contain the spread of Communism in the newly established Soviet Union under Stalin. But when Hitler invaded the Soviet Union, Churchill knew that Hitler was a far worse enemy than Stalin. Churchill realized he would have to work together with Stalin in order to defeat

Germany. He sent British troops to help defend the Soviet Union, and in October 1944 Churchill traveled to Moscow to meet with Stalin and other Soviet leaders.

In June 1944 the Allied forces invaded Normandy and forced the Nazis back into Germany. On May 7, 1945, the Allies accepted Germany's surrender. May 8 was named Victory in Europe Day, or V-E Day. Churchill broadcast the news over the radio. He told the crowd that had gathered at Whitehall in London, "This is your victory."

The Japanese were given terms of surrender a few months after that, on August 14. They formally surrendered a few weeks later, on September 2. World War II was over.

Remains of a bombed London bank in 1943

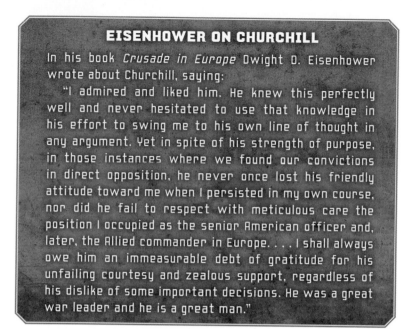

EISENHOWER ON CHURCHILL

In his book *Crusade in Europe* Dwight D. Eisenhower wrote about Churchill, saying:

"I admired and liked him. He knew this perfectly well and never hesitated to use that knowledge in his effort to swing me to his own line of thought in any argument. Yet in spite of his strength of purpose, in those instances where we found our convictions in direct opposition, he never once lost his friendly attitude toward me when I persisted in my own course, nor did he fail to respect with meticulous care the position I occupied as the senior American officer and, later, the Allied commander in Europe. . . . I shall always owe him an immeasurable debt of gratitude for his unfailing courtesy and zealous support, regardless of his dislike of some important decisions. He was a great war leader and he is a great man."

A SECOND TERM

Despite the recent victory and his success at leading the country through the war, Churchill lost his campaign for reelection as prime minister in 1945, but spent the next six years as the leader of the opposition. That meant his political party was not in charge of the government. As the opposing party leader, Churchill still had a lot of authority. He continued to speak about politics. His biggest concern was Communism again. He was afraid that, with Germany gone, the Soviet Union would begin to conquer in its place.

Churchill had actually suggested that Britain and the United States would need to attack Soviet troops as soon as the war ended, to keep them from occupying former German lands, but the British chiefs of staff had declared the plan unfeasible. He urged both Britain and the United States not to relax, but to stay alert and to watch the Soviet Union closely. He also encouraged Britain to align itself more closely with the United States and not as strongly with the rest of Europe.

In 1951 the political current shifted and Churchill's party took control of the government. He became prime minister again. He spent the majority of his time trying to keep Britain from losing its military strength or its remaining colonies. Churchill also maintained his link with the United States, working closely with the new American president, Dwight D. Eisenhower, who took office in 1953.

A MAN OF ART AND LETTERS

Churchill was not only a writer, he was a painter. He often painted when he was depressed, and especially during his "wilderness years." Many of his paintings were landscapes done during his vacations to places like Egypt, Morocco, and the south of France.

Churchill was far better known for his writing, however.

In 1900 he published his only novel, *Savrola*. Over the course of his life, he also wrote two biographies (one on his father, Lord Randolph, and the other on one of his ancestors, the first Duke of Marlborough), three sets of **memoirs**, several histories, and a great many newspaper and magazine

Churchill and Eisenhower in 1951

articles. His most famous article appeared in the *Evening Standard* in 1936 and warned of the rise of Hitler and the danger in trying to appease him and allowing him to rearm Germany. His most famous books are probably the six-volume memoir *The Second World War* and the four-volume history *A History of the English-Speaking Peoples*.

In 1953 Churchill received the Nobel Prize in Literature "for his mastery of historical and biographical description as well as for brilliant oratory in defending exalted human values." He is the only British prime minister to ever receive that award. His speeches have been collected into dozens of volumes, including *The Unrelenting Struggle*, *The Dawn of Liberation*, and *Victory*.

LATER YEARS

Churchill had suffered a mild **stroke** in 1949 while vacationing in France. He had a second stroke in June 1953. After resting at Chartwell, his country home in England, Churchill returned in October to speak at a Conservative Party conference. He had not fully recovered, however, and knew he would never be the same physically or mentally. He resigned his post as prime minister in 1955, appointing Anthony Eden as his successor. Officially Churchill remained a member of Parliament until 1964, when he did not seek reelection. Queen Elizabeth II offered to make him duke of London, but Churchill's son, Randolph, argued that he did not want to inherit that title, and so Churchill declined the honor. He spent most of his time at his home at Chartwell or at his London house in Hyde Park Gate, and struggled with depression more often as his body and mind failed him.

Churchill (middle) with his son, Randolph (left), and grandson, Winston (right)

On January 10, 1965, Churchill suffered a massive stroke. He died two weeks later, on January 24. He was ninety years old. It was also the seventieth anniversary of his father's death. Churchill had lived to twice Lord Randolph's age.

Queen Elizabeth ordered a state funeral for Churchill, and his body lay in state for three days at the Palace of Westminster before the service was held in St. Paul's Cathedral. More statesmen attended than at any previous funeral in history. Churchill was buried in his family's plot at St. Martin's Church, Bladon, in Woodstock, not far from Blenheim Palace, where he had been born.

Churchill was one of the first world leaders to worry about Germany's plans, and to warn against Hitler's ambitions. His courage and determination helped guide Britain through the war, and helped unite the Allied forces that ultimately defeated the Nazi advance.

JOSEF STALIN

JOSEF STALIN was a powerful ruler of the Soviet Union. He expanded the country's territories and power and began the campaign of Communist expansion that led to the Cold War with the United States. His nonaggression pact with Hitler allowed Nazi Germany to begin World War II, but when Stalin changed sides and joined the Allied forces, his support helped end the war.

EARLY LIFE

Josef Vissarionovich Stalin was born Ioseb (or Josef) Besarionis dze Jughashvili in Gori, Georgia, on December 18, 1878 (some historians believe he was in fact born in 1879). His father, Besarion Jughashvili, was a boot maker. His mother, Ekaterina Geladze, washed clothes and linens to make money. Stalin was their third child, but both of his older brothers had died as infants.

Stalin's mother, Ekaterina Geladze

Besarion owned his own workshop and made decent money. Then he started to drink too much. Eventually he lost his business. Besarion also became violent toward Stalin and his mother. The family moved several times, and lived in complete poverty.

When Stalin was not yet seven, he contracted smallpox, a dangerous

Stalin as a child in Georgia

disease that often killed small children. Stalin survived but the illness left his face badly scarred for the rest of his life. When he got older he altered photographs to hide the damage. The other children picked on Stalin, laughing at his scars and mocking his poor family. He often got into fights.

EDUCATION

When Stalin was ten his mother managed to get him into the local church school, the Gori theological school. Stalin did very well there and earned top marks. He was also an excellent singer and sometimes earned money by singing at weddings. Unfortunately Stalin's father did not approve of the boy's singing or his religious education. Besarion began drinking more heavily. Eventually Stalin's father got himself into trouble. He got into a fight at the local tavern, smashed the windows, and even attacked the town's chief of police. The police did not arrest Besarion, but they did tell him to leave town. He moved to Tiflis and got a job at

Stalin in 1894

a shoe factory there. Stalin and his mother stayed behind in Gori.

Around this same time a horse-drawn carriage hit Stalin. The accident permanently injured his left arm. A second carriage hit Stalin a few years later. This time the damage was so severe he was taken to a hospital in Tiflis. His father found Stalin there and stole him away. Besarion tried to make the boy an **apprentice** at the shoe factory. But Stalin's mother found out and took Stalin. She brought him back to Gori to finish his education.

In 1894 Stalin graduated at the top of his class. He even won a scholarship to the Tiflis Theological Seminary. He did very well there as well, but joined a secret organization of Georgian **patriots**. The patriots wanted Georgia to become an independent nation from Russia. They did not appreciate the school's attempts to make them learn Russian language and culture. Through this group Stalin learned about Karl Marx, who had created the philosophy of Communism. In August 1898 Stalin joined the Russian Social-Democratic Labor Party, or SD.

In 1899 Stalin was technically expelled from Tiflis for missing his final exams. His mother stated that he had been ill. He later claimed the real reason was his attempts to convert his fellow students to Marxism.

DANGEROUS VIEWS

Stalin's education had prepared him for the priesthood. But without passing the final exams he could not continue that career. Instead he got a job as a clerk at the Tiflis Meteorological Observatory and may have tutored children in private lessons. Stalin also continued the **revolutionary** work he had begun in school. He spent much of his time organizing strikes and leading demonstrations. The Okhrana, the Russian Empire's secret police, arrested SD party leaders on April 3, 1901, but Stalin escaped and went underground. Now he was a full-time revolutionary. He wrote articles for the radical newspaper *Brdzola* (which means "Struggle"). For money he lived off donations from friends and party members.

Stalin
around
age 20

In October Stalin got a job at an oil refinery in Batumi. A fire broke out there the following year. The rich owners refused to pay their workers a bonus for handling the fire, though. They suspected someone had set it deliberately. Stalin organized a number of strikes in protest. The strikes led to fights and several deaths. The authorities arrested Stalin on April 18, 1902. They couldn't find enough evidence to prove he had started the riots, but they held him for over a year anyway.

An imperial police card on Stalin

Then they **exiled** him to Siberia for three years instead of sending him to prison. There was no need. Siberia was so far away that he couldn't cause any trouble from there. He reached Novaya Uda in Siberia on December 9, 1903.

The Social-Democratic Labor Party had held a meeting in London a few months before. The party's two leaders, Julius Martov and Vladimir Lenin, had argued. They wound up splitting the party into Lenin's Bolsheviks and Martov's Mensheviks. The Mensheviks felt success required a large group of activists and revolutionaries. The Bolsheviks believed a small group of true revolutionaries and a large group of supporters was better. Stalin sided with the Bolsheviks.

Stalin managed to obtain false identification papers

while in Novaya Uda. On January 17, 1904, he broke his exile by boarding a train for Tiflis. Once he was back home he returned to organizing strikes and demonstrations. He started using the name Stalin instead of his given name, Jughashvili, to throw off the secret police. *Stalin* means "man of steel."

Stalin spent the next two years rallying his native Georgia against both Russia and the Mensheviks. He also met his first wife, Ekaterina Svanidze, during that time. Stalin married Svanidze on July 28, 1905. Their son, Yakov, was born on March 18, 1907.

In December 1905 Stalin and two others from Georgia were elected to attend the Bolshevik conference in Finland in January. Stalin met Lenin there for the first time. In 1907 Stalin and Lenin attended the fifth SD party meeting in London. While there Stalin encountered his future rival Leon Trotsky for the first time. After the conference, Stalin began to focus less on Menshevik-controlled Georgia and more on Russia itself.

Stalin moved his family to Baku

Stalin's son, Joseph

in 1907, but his wife became ill from the pollution there. She died of **tuberculosis** that November. Stalin spent several months in mourning and sent Yakov away to his wife's family. Stalin threw himself into his work. The Okhrana arrested him in March 1908 and sentenced him to two years in Siberia for stirring up political unrest. Stalin escaped again a few months later. He was arrested several more times over the next few years, but escaped each time.

In January 1912, Lenin left the SD party for good and formed an independent Bolshevik Party. Stalin moved to Saint Petersburg to take charge of the Bolshevik weekly newspaper, *Zvezda*. He renamed it *Pravda* and turned it into a daily paper. The first issue was published on May 5 (April 22 by the old Russian calendar).

Stalin was captured again in February 1913, and sent to Siberia once more. This time he spent several years in the cold wasteland, and fathered two children with a young woman named Lidia

Stalin in uniform around 1915

Pereprygina. He was then drafted into the army in late 1916 but was found unfit because of his injured left arm.

PARTY LINE

In February 1917 the Bolsheviks removed the Russian tsar and replaced him with a temporary new government. The new government's leaders were all from the former imperial parliament, however. They had different goals from the Bolsheviks and wanted to stay involved in World War I. The Bolsheviks felt Russia should quit the war and concentrate on its own people. In October they overthrew the temporary government and took control of the country themselves, forming the new Communist Party and the Soviet Union.

Stalin helped Lenin organize the takeover, which became known as the October Revolution. Stalin continued by helping Lenin escape capture from rivals during those months. He also took control of the Bolsheviks while Lenin was in hiding. He was made commissar for nationalities as a reward. The position gave him tremendous authority.

Stalin was now responsible for keeping the country's non-Russian citizens from causing trouble. He quickly took control of the military and intimidated the soldiers into obeying orders. In 1922 he became general secretary and moved many of his friends and supporters into key government positions. He also removed many of Trotsky's supporters to weaken his longtime rival.

When Lenin suffered a stroke in 1922, Stalin became Lenin's contact with the rest of the world. He spoke on Lenin's behalf. That meant Stalin was effectively the new head of the government. He and Lenin argued frequently, however. Lenin felt Stalin was too quick to use violence to solve problems. Lenin began to realize Stalin's full ambitions, and actually wrote to Trotsky. He suggested they work together to limit Stalin's power and prevent him from taking control of the party and the country. The document was called Lenin's Testament. Stalin had formed alliances of his own, however. He and his allies stopped party members from reading Lenin's Testament at the Communist Party meeting in April 1923. Lenin died on January 21, 1924. Stalin, along with Grigory Zinoviev and Lev Kamenev, was now in charge of the party. Stalin removed Trotsky from the Central Committee and finally from the party itself. After that was done, he turned on Zinoviev and Kamenev. He stripped them of their positions as well. Stalin was now completely in control.

Vladimir Lenin

LENIN'S CONCERNS

Lenin wrote in his Testament:

"Comrade Stalin, having become General Secretary, has concentrated enormous power in his hands, and I am not sure that he always knows how to use that power with sufficient caution. . . . I therefore propose to our comrades to consider a means of removing Stalin from this post and appointing someone else who differs from Stalin in one weighty respect: being more tolerant, more loyal, more polite, more considerate of his comrades."

FIVE-YEAR PLAN

In 1928 Stalin had introduced a Five-Year Plan to industrialize the new Soviet Union. With this plan, the government increased coal and iron production and electrical

Stalin's second wife and their daughter

generation. Overseers compiled files on each worker. They publicly humiliated those who did not meet production goals. Poor workers could even be accused of sabotage and shot or put to manual labor. At the same time, Stalin increased the pay for **skilled labor**, as opposed to common labor. That created a gap between the two groups, and established new classes in the Soviet Union.

TERROR TACTICS

By 1932 Stalin's opponents were growing more vocal. They were complaining about his Five-Year Plan and the methods he was using to encourage hard work. They were not happy about the increased wages or the new class system. Many politicians felt they had been wrong to remove Trotsky from power. Stalin tried to silence his critics, but his own **protégé**, Sergey Kirov, protested and won the support of the Politburo, the Soviet congress. Kirov was winning more and more approval from party members, and Stalin worried that Kirov would try to replace him as leader.

Kirov was assassinated on December 1, 1934. Stalin claimed a **conspiracy** was behind the death. He used Kirov's death as an excuse to arrest and execute several of his rivals, including Kamenev and Zinoviev.

In September 1936, Stalin appointed his follower Nikolai Yezhov to run the NKVD, the Communist secret police. Yezhov soon arrested all of Stalin's chief rivals and critics. The NKVD convinced these prisoners to confess to treason, and then executed them. Next they purged the Soviet army of anyone they thought was a traitor. This

included eight commanders who were charged with con-
spiring with Germany.

Finally, in 1938, Stalin announced that Fascists (people
who believed in Fascism, which teaches that a country
needs a single strong leader and should be run like a business) had taken control of the secret police. They were the
ones responsible for all these deaths. He appointed Lavrenti
Beria to head the secret police and find out who was
responsible. Beria captured and executed all of the other
high-ranking officers in the NKVD, including Yezhov. All
those who had known about the purging of potential rivals
and Stalin's involvement with them were now dead. Nearly
seven hundred thousand people died during what became
known as the Great Purge.

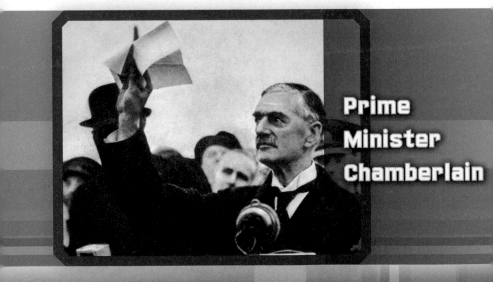

Prime Minister Chamberlain

NONAGGRESSION

Stalin did not trust Adolf Hitler or his plans for Germany. He recognized the führer's strong ambitions and the danger an active Germany could represent. But Stalin was not sure he could stand against Germany on his own. Instead he suggested an antifascist alliance between the Soviet Union, Britain, and France.

Unfortunately, the British prime minister, Neville Chamberlain, did not agree. He didn't trust Stalin enough to form an alliance with him. Winston Churchill actually agreed with Stalin, however. Churchill was strongly anti-Marxist and had worked hard to control Soviet power during and after the Russian Civil War. But he felt that Germany was a bigger immediate threat and that they could not prevent the Nazis from controlling Europe without Russia's help. But Churchill was outvoted, and Britain refused the Soviet Union's suggestion.

Stalin felt he had only two choices left. He could stand against Germany alone and possibly be crushed. Or he could work something out with Germany instead. He opened talks with Hitler. On August 23, 1939, the Soviet Union and Nazi Germany signed a nonaggression pact. The two countries agreed not to attack each other. They negotiated a secret second arrangement that divided eastern Europe between

German and Soviet control. Each nation agreed not to inter-fere with the areas marked as the other's territory.

A few days later, on September 1, 1939, Germany invaded western Poland and began World War II. The Red Army, or Soviet army, invaded eastern Poland on September 17. Soon the two nations had split Poland between them.

Stalin took control of Lithuania, Latvia, and Estonia in June 1940. He added those three nations to the Soviet Union. He tried to invade Finland as well, but was forced back. Ultimately he claimed only a small portion of Finland's eastern region.

In October 1940 Germany, Japan, and Italy signed a **Tripartite** Pact agreeing to defend one another against attack and to stay out of one another's way. Stalin then contacted the German foreign minister to discuss a more permanent arrangement between Germany and the Soviet Union. The Soviet Union was presented with a writ-ten agreement for Axis entry in late November. Stalin requested a few revisions. Germany did not reply.

On June 22, 1941, Hitler attacked several Soviet-held territories. The pact with the Soviet Union was over.

ALLIED STANCE

Stalin had suspected Germany would attack him sooner

or later. He had not expected an attack until Germany defeated Britain, however, because fighting a war on two fronts was foolish. In April 1941 Churchill sent Stalin a message warning that German troop movements suggested they would attack the Soviet Union soon. Stalin did not trust Churchill, and ignored the warning. Hitler's attack caught him and the Soviet troops by surprise.

Germany sent three million men and over three thousand tanks into the Soviet Union in three groups: one toward Saint Petersburg, then called Leningrad; one toward Moscow; and one toward the Ukraine. They captured the city of Minsk and slaughtered its people. That only made the Soviets more determined to fight, however. So did the fact that Stalin had shot several of Minsk's senior officers for failing to protect the city. Clearly, surrender and retreat were not options.

The Germans advanced rapidly and surrounded Kiev, Ukraine. Stalin ordered his troops to stay in place. The Germans did finally take the Ukraine capital, but the delay cost them several months. Winter was now upon them. The Nazis were not prepared for the brutal cold. They also had no way to get food and ammunition this deep into the Soviet Union. Soviet forces began to pick away at them. Meanwhile, Stalin had formed a pact with Britain and the other Allies.

He started receiving aid and supplies from them.

By October the Germans had reached Moscow. Stalin ordered an evacuation, but he remained behind to oversee the war effort. The Germans kept attacking, but they could not take the city. On December 6 the Red Army launched a counterattack. They took the Nazis by surprise and forced them to retreat. By January the Russians had pushed the Germans back two hundred miles.

In 1942 the Germans advanced again. This time they concentrated on the oil fields to the south. That also put them near Volgograd, which had been renamed Stalingrad in Stalin's honor. He insisted that the Red Army hold the city at any cost. Stalin drafted over a million Soviet soldiers for the fight. They held against the Germans in November, and then cut off the German supplies. The German field

Stalin, Roosevelt, and Churchill at the Tehran Conference

marshal surrendered in early February 1943. Stalingrad was safe, and the Soviet army had halted the German advance for good.

In November 1943 Stalin met with Winston Churchill and Franklin

D. Roosevelt in Teheran, Iran. They discussed military strategy and their plans for postwar Europe. They were all confident now that they could defeat the Nazis. Stalin wanted his new allies to open a second front in Europe to split the Nazi forces. The western leaders had promised to land troops in western Europe in 1942 but had not done so. They finally agreed to launch a new offensive in the spring of 1944. That attack began in June, on what became known as D-day.

In October 1944 Churchill traveled to Moscow to speak with Stalin. The British prime minister worried about the Soviet Union's increasing power after the war. He agreed to leave Romania and Bulgaria under Soviet influence but argued that Yugoslavia and Hungary should be shared among the Allies. He and Stalin also argued about Poland. Stalin agreed to negotiate with Polish leaders, but said he would not allow a Polish government that was actively hostile toward him.

Stalin, Churchill, and Roosevelt met again in Yalta, Ukraine, in February 1945. Soviet troops covered most of eastern Europe. Stalin resisted the others' requests for him to withdraw after the war. He did agree to allow free elections in those countries, however. Stalin also convinced the others that eastern Germany fell within Soviet control. He agreed to consider an independent government for Poland

Churchill, Roosevelt, and Stalin at the Yalta Conference

if it was pro-Communist enough to not pose a threat. He also promised to enter the war against Japan three months after Germany's final defeat. In return, he wanted back the land Russia had lost in the Russo-Japanese War in 1904.

At this same meeting Stalin, Churchill, and Roosevelt agreed that the old League of Nations (which had been created after World War I) was no longer effective. But they still felt it was important for the countries of the world to meet and work together. They decided to form a new organization of united nations instead. The United Nations would work to keep peace around the world.

After Hitler committed suicide on April 30, 1945, German forces surrendered a few days later. The Allied leaders met again at Potsdam, Germany, in July 1945, but Roosevelt had passed away in April. His former vice president, Harry S. Truman, was now president. At the same time, Churchill's Conservative Party lost the British elections and the Labor Party's Clement Attlee took over as Britain's chief negotiator. Truman informed Stalin and Attlee that the United States was going to use a powerful new bomb against Japan. Hiroshima and Nagasaki were bombed in August and Japan surrendered soon after. The Soviet Union never joined the battle against Japan. That meant they did not retrieve their lost land as a reward. World War II was over.

AFTER THE WAR

Stalin didn't waste time consolidating his power. He set up Communist **regimes** in Romania, Bulgaria, Hungary, East Germany, Poland, and Czechoslovakia. Now Communist states stood between the Soviet Union and western Europe. Churchill referred to this as an "Iron Curtain" that blocked the west from Moscow. The new Communist nations were also called the Eastern or Soviet bloc. Their presence made Britain and the United States uneasy enough to form the North Atlantic Treaty Organization, or **NATO**.

In 1948 Stalin tried to take complete control of Berlin. The other Allies **airlifted** supplies and forced him to back down. Stalin did, however, support the creation of the Jewish state that same year. He was one of the first to officially recognize Israel.

In 1950 Stalin signed the Sino-Soviet Treaty of Friendship and Alliance. The agreement allied the Soviet Union with the People's Republic of China. That same year Stalin encouraged North Korea's Communist ruler Kim Il Sung to invade South Korea. He hoped Kim Il Sung would transform Korea into a united Communist state. But the United Nations voted to send troops to defend South Korea. The Soviet Union was on the UN Security Council. It could have vetoed the decision to help South Korea. But Stalin was **boycotting** the UN at the time. The Korean War lasted until 1953. Stalin's actions caused a wave of anticommunism in the United States and increased hostility between the two countries.

Poster of Stalin

At home Stalin was still considered a hero of the people for uniting the nation and for defeating the invading Nazis. He continued to control the

Communist Party and the Soviet Union with an iron fist.

FINAL REST

Stalin's health had begun to deteriorate by the 1950s. On March 1, 1953, he suffered a stroke that paralyzed half of his body. He died a few days later, on March 5. The cause of his death was listed as a cerebral hemorrhage. Stalin's body was then placed in Lenin's mausoleum, next to his former friend and mentor. Stalin's successor, Nikita Khrushchev, quickly denounced Stalin's regime and worked hard to reform Soviet policies. He also revealed the brutalities of Stalin's rule, including his purges and terror campaigns. Stalin went from being a hero to a villain in a matter of years. Every trace of him was removed wherever possible. Even his body was eventually relocated and buried next to the Kremlin's walls. This was a way of showing that Stalin was not considered good enough to be buried near Lenin.

Stalin was a powerful dictator who consolidated his power and formed a strong, aggressive Soviet Union. His atrocities are well remembered, but without his help the Allies might never have defeated Nazi Germany.

Bust of Stalin in the Museum of Communism, Czech Republic

FRANKLIN D. ROOSEVELT

FRANKLIN D. ROOSEVELT, often referred to as FDR, was the president of the United States during World War II. He brought the country out of the Great Depression and into the war, making America a superpower and one of the most influential nations in the world.

EARLY LIFE

Franklin Delano Roosevelt was born in Hyde Park, New York, on January 30, 1882. His father, James Roosevelt, and his mother, Sara Ann Delano, were both from wealthy New York families. His mother's family had come to America on the *Mayflower*—some of the first and most prestigious settlers in the United States.

Roosevelt grew up with everything a child could need or want. He was an only child and his mother coddled him, though she tried her best not to spoil him. His father was older and not as concerned about keeping the boy in line; he always made sure Roosevelt had the best of everything and enjoyed his son's company. Roosevelt learned German and

Roosevelt on his father's shoulder in 1883

French at an early age. He traveled to Europe frequently, even as a child. He learned to ride, shoot, row, and play both polo and lawn tennis. He also learned how to play golf as a teenager. He even became club champion at the Campobello Island club near his family's summer home in New Brunswick, Canada. Unfortunately, a mysterious illness forced Roosevelt to give up the sport. We still don't

Roosevelt on his first pony

know exactly what happened because throughout his life, Roosevelt never wanted to reveal the details of his health.

EDUCATION

Roosevelt received most of his early education from his mother, various nannies, and private tutors. When he was fourteen, however, his parents sent him to the prestigious Groton Preparatory School in Massachusetts. Roosevelt did well at the boarding school. The headmaster, Endicott Peabody, often preached about a Christian's duty to help the less fortunate. He urged his students to enter public service. That message stayed with Roosevelt his entire life. During this time Roosevelt also grew close to his distant cousin, Theodore Roosevelt. Theodore was a promising young politician at that time.

After graduating from Groton, Roosevelt entered Harvard. He joined the Alpha Delta Phi fraternity and became president of the *Harvard Crimson*, the daily campus newspaper. Theodore Roosevelt became president of the United States, and Franklin Roosevelt's permanent role model, during this time. The younger Roosevelt admired his dashing cousin's style and his enthusiasm for reform. At a New York horse show in 1902, followed by a White House reception that New Year's, Roosevelt

Roosevelt (center front) as president of the *Harvard Crimson*

met another distant cousin, Theodore's niece Eleanor. Roosevelt and Eleanor took an immediate liking to each other. He began to court her soon after.

Roosevelt graduated from Harvard in 1904 and continued on to Columbia Law School. He passed the New York State bar exam in 1907, and was licensed to practice law in New York.

MARRIAGE

Franklin and Eleanor married in New York City in 1905. Unlike their mutual cousin President Roosevelt, the young couple were both Democrats. All three of them

Franklin and Eleanor in 1906

Franklin and
Eleanor with Anna,
James, and Elliot

shared a strong interest in politics, however. Theodore walked Eleanor down the aisle in place of his deceased brother, her father. The newlyweds moved into his family's estate at Springwood. Their first child, Anna Eleanor, was born in 1906, and their second, James, in 1907. Their third child, Franklin Delano, Jr., was born in March 1909, but died of **influenza** that November. The following year saw Elliott's birth. Then the Roosevelts had a second Franklin Delano, Jr., in 1914 and finally John Aspinwall in 1916. Eleanor was not as interested in having a social presence as her husband was. She spent much of her time over those years staying home and caring for all their children, though she did have nurses and nannies to assist her.

NAVAL DUTY

In 1908 Roosevelt accepted a job at the respected New York City Wall Street law firm Carter Ledyard & Milburn. The firm specialized in corporate law. Roosevelt decided his true interests lay in politics, however. In 1910 he was elected to the New York Senate. Roosevelt opposed Tammany Hall, a group of New York politicians that controlled most of New York City politics from the 1790s through the 1930s. The Tammany Hall members believed in making themselves and their friends rich and powerful. Roosevelt helped prevent them from electing their choice to the Senate and won the respect of his fellow New York Democrats in the process. Roosevelt was reelected in 1912, but he accepted an appointment from the U.S. Senate as assistant U.S. secretary of the navy and gave up his Senate seat. The following year he ran for the U.S. Senate but his Tammany-backed opponent defeated him.

Roosevelt served as assistant secretary of the navy for seven years. He helped expand the navy and found the U.S. Navy Reserve. He also worked to make sure the country's naval plants and shipyards were running smoothly. Once World War I began Roosevelt helped create plans to battle the German U-boats in the North Sea. He was an enthusiastic supporter of the submarine and other naval innovations. Roosevelt met Winston Churchill for the first time during a 1918 tour of American naval facilities in Britain and France.

The war ended that same year. Roosevelt was put in charge of the navy's demobilization, which is the process of returning the ships to the United States and helping

Roosevelt as assistant secretary of the navy in 1918

those who were drafted return to their own lives. It was a long and difficult process. Roosevelt resigned his post in July 1920. That same year, however, Democratic presidential candidate James Cox invited Roosevelt to serve as his running mate. Cox was the governor of Ohio. He hoped that New York–born Roosevelt would help him win votes along the East Coast. Unfortunately, the Republican candidate, Warren G. Harding, easily defeated the pair.

LIMITED MOBILITY

In August 1921 the Roosevelts were at their summer home on Campobello Island in New Brunswick, Canada, for vacation. Roosevelt fell ill with what doctors thought was poliomyelitis, or polio. Polio was a common illness at the time, and the symptoms seemed to match that illness. More recently, however, doctors have suggested that he may have had Guillain-Barré Syndrome instead. This disease was far less common and not as well known, even among doctors.

For several days Roosevelt had a high fever and became paralyzed from the chest down. Over the course of the next month he saw several doctors and spent time in the hospital. He slowly recovered the use of his upper body, but remained paralyzed from the waist down for the rest of his life.

Roosevelt refused to let this sudden disability stop him. He got iron braces for his hips and legs. Then he learned to walk short distances by supporting himself with a cane and swiveling his torso to move his lower body. He refused to use a wheelchair in public. When he had to stand up, his aides or one of his sons supported him. Roosevelt had a car designed with special hand controls so he could drive even though he couldn't use his feet.

POLITICAL DEPRESSION

In 1922 Roosevelt helped his friend Alfred E. Smith become governor of New York. Smith ran for president in 1924 and lost, but ran again in 1928 against Herbert Hoover. Smith suggested to Roosevelt that he run for New York State governor. Smith lost the presidential election, even in New York, but Roosevelt won the race for governor.

In October 1929 the Wall Street stock market crashed. People who had money invested in stocks lost a fortune. A lot of people lost their life savings and businesses collapsed.

It created the worst economic depression in American history. President Hoover didn't do enough to solve the problem. He refused to help the unemployed in cities and vetoed a bill to create a federal unemployment agency. He didn't provide relief for farmers quickly enough to help most of them save their homes and their farms. He also opposed several public works projects that could have created more jobs. Roosevelt did the best he could for his own state. In 1930 he won his bid for reelection, though he was forced to rely upon Tammany Hall for support. During his second term he set up the New York State Temporary Emergency Relief Administration and provided help for the unemployed and the elderly. He also limited work hours and created several public works projects.

By 1932 the Great Depression had only gotten worse. Hoover was not getting the job done. For the next presidential election, the Democrats turned to Roosevelt. When he accepted the nomination, Roosevelt said, "I pledge myself, to a new deal for the American people. This is more than a political campaign. It is a call to arms."

With his running mate, Texas politician John Nance Garner, Roosevelt campaigned for a "New Deal." He also appealed to the poor, the minorities, and the working-class laborers—the people the Depression had hit hardest. Roosevelt won 57 percent of the vote and carried all but

THE STOCK MARKET CRASH OF 1929

The 1920s were known as the Roaring Twenties in the United States. Everything was going great. People were getting rich and spending money like crazy. Everyone thought the party would never end.

Unfortunately, that meant most people weren't careful with their money. They thought they could always make more, so they spent it all quickly. People drove fancy cars, lived in big houses, wore expensive clothes, and didn't bother to save any money for later. Because everyone was buying so much, prices everywhere rose rapidly.

By 1929 the prices had become more than most people could afford. Suddenly people realized that they had no money set aside for a rainy day. They had nothing to live on if they lost their jobs. And they couldn't afford to buy fancy things or even regular things anymore.

People around the country started to panic. And the stock market reflected that. The prices of stocks rose and fell with people's confidence in companies that sold things like steel, cotton, timber, orange juice, and other goods. Traders could buy and sell shares of companies that sold these goods all over the world. How much stock they bought and sold affected the price of that stock.

By September buyers were hesitating. They couldn't afford to buy stock and then lose money if the stock prices fell. That hesitation caused the prices to fall quickly.

October 24 became known as Black Thursday. Investors started selling their stocks so they wouldn't lose more money. Stock prices dropped rapidly. More people panicked and sold stocks. The prices fell further. In two weeks the stock market lost over thirty billion dollars in value. People who had been rich were now broke. And everyone across the country felt the crash. The entire economy collapsed into a depression.

six states. Americans had spoken, and they had said they wanted Franklin D. Roosevelt as their president.

TURNING THE TIDE

Roosevelt took office on March 4, 1933, thirty-two days after Hitler became chancellor of Germany. The United States was in the worst shape it had ever been. At least a quarter of its workforce was unemployed. Crop prices had fallen by 40 to 60 percent. Industrial production had been cut in half. Over two million people were homeless. Banks in thirty-two states had closed their doors. Roosevelt quickly instituted a program of "relief, recovery, and reform."

First he sent a number of bills through Congress. He started with the Emergency Banking Act to help the banks reopen. He began the Federal Emergency Relief Administration and hired 250,000 young men to the Civilian Conservation Corps to work on rural projects. The Reconstruction Finance Corporation, which started under President Hoover, helped finance railroads and industry. That meant people were given jobs again. The Home Owners' Refinancing Act created the Home Owners' Loan Corporation, which provided mortgage relief for farmers and home owners. The Agricultural Adjustment Administration paid farmers to leave some of their land empty. That raised the price of their remaining crops.

Roosevelt passed the National Industrial Recovery Act and established the National Recovery Administration to make industries establish codes of conduct, noncompete agreements, minimum prices, and other regulations. But the Supreme Court later ruled the act unconstitutional. Roosevelt managed to pass several other reform bills, however, including one to create the Securities and Exchange Commission in 1934. The commission was designed to control spending on Wall Street and prevent another stock market crash.

Roosevelt spent federal money to create dams and power stations and other public works. This created jobs and stimulated the economy. He repealed prohibition (which had made alcohol illegal) to create new tax revenue. He modernized agriculture in areas like the Tennessee Valley. At the same time, he cut federal spending in several other places, including federal salaries, research, and education.

During all of this, Roosevelt kept the American people informed. He started a series of radio broadcasts called fireside chats in which he talked directly to the people and told them what was happening. The information, and the fact that the president himself was taking time to keep them informed, helped ease everyone's fears across the country.

By 1935 Roosevelt was ready to begin a second wave of New Deal measures. He set up a national relief agency and started Social Security (a government program that pays Americans a pension once they retire). He established the right to organize unions and strike for better working conditions. The business community did not appreciate these new reforms, but the American people did. Roosevelt won reelection by a landslide in 1936.

In 1940 Roosevelt ran for a third term. No one had ever done this before. There was no formal rule against it, but George Washington had turned down a third term. Ever since then, presidents had limited themselves to two. But Roosevelt wanted to continue the work he'd begun. He ran again and won the election with 55 percent of the popular vote and thirty-eight of the forty-eight states.

Roosevelt in Jamestown, North Dakota, in 1936

GOOD NEIGHBORS

Roosevelt was determined to focus on the United States' problems ahead of other nations'. The country did not have the energy or the resources to deal with other nations' problems. Because of that, in 1933 Roosevelt began what he called the Good Neighbor Policy. The United States had maintained soldiers in Latin American countries like Haiti, Cuba, and Panama. He removed those troops, but agreed to still keep an eye on Latin America and impose **economic sanctions**, or penalties, when necessary. But going forward, the United States would no longer send troops to intervene in local conflicts.

This new policy extended to the rest of the world as well. Roosevelt did not want to completely isolate the United States. He knew the country needed to stay involved in world politics to maintain good trade relations overseas. But he did not want to commit the United States to a war across the ocean. When Germany and Japan began to seek dominance in Europe and Asia, Roosevelt did not let the United States become directly involved. He watched as Japan took **Manchuria** in 1931, Mussolini's Italy took Ethiopia in 1935, and Nazis took over the Rhineland in 1936. In 1938 Hitler took control of Austria. At the Munich conference that same year, Britain and France agreed to let Germany take over the Sudetenland in the hopes of avoiding a war. Roosevelt did not approve, but the United States could not get involved. Congress had passed the Johnson Act in 1934. That act prevented the government from loaning money to nations that still owed the United States money from World War I. The Neutrality Act of 1935 meant the United States could not send arms or ammunition to foreign nations at war. And the Neutrality Act of 1937 banned American citizens from entering war zones or taking ships owned by warring nations.

Roosevelt still watched Germany, Italy, and Japan carefully. In 1939 he asked Congress to repeal the Neutrality Act. He wanted to sell arms to European countries opposing Hitler. Congress refused. That September Germany invaded Poland and began World War II. Roosevelt returned to Congress. On November 4 it passed the Pittman Bill, which allowed the United States to sell weapons to other nations if they could pay in cash.

At the same time, Roosevelt quietly got the United States ready for battle. He increased the defense budget. He appointed pro-war and anti-Nazi officials to his cabinet and to lead positions in the navy and the War Department. When France fell to Germany in May 1940, Roosevelt began writing to the British prime minister, Winston Churchill. The Neutrality Act still prevented Roosevelt from sending help directly. He did trade fifty U.S. destroyers for several British bases in the Caribbean and Newfoundland. Churchill needed more help, but at least it gave Britain a bit more firepower.

Germany, Italy, and Japan signed the Tripartite Pact on September 27, 1940. Part of their agreement was to defend one another against American attack. They had hoped to force the United States to remain neutral. Instead, their stance showed their aggression against the United States. That allowed Roosevelt to condemn them and their ambitions for world conquest.

In March 1941 Roosevelt convinced Congress to pass the Lend-Lease Act. The United States could now lend war materials to the Allies and accept payment after the war was over. Shipments to Britain began days after the bill was signed. Roosevelt also took steps to protect Greenland and Iceland. He even authorized the navy to attack German submarines if they passed too close to American waters. On August 14 Congress narrowly approved the Selective Service Act. That allowed the government to draft soldiers, even in peacetime. That same day, Roosevelt and Churchill announced the Atlantic Charter. The document stated that all nations should be allowed to determine their own governments without outside interference. It was Roosevelt's way of saying what Germany was doing was wrong and had to be stopped.

On September 4, 1941, the U.S. destroyer *Greer* exchanged

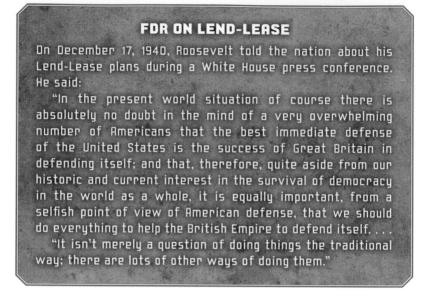

FDR ON LEND-LEASE

On December 17, 1940, Roosevelt told the nation about his Lend-Lease plans during a White House press conference. He said:

"In the present world situation of course there is absolutely no doubt in the mind of a very overwhelming number of Americans that the best immediate defense of the United States is the success of Great Britain in defending itself; and that, therefore, quite aside from our historic and current interest in the survival of democracy in the world as a whole, it is equally important, from a selfish point of view of American defense, that we should do everything to help the British Empire to defend itself. . . .

"It isn't merely a question of doing things the traditional way; there are lots of other ways of doing them."

fire with a German sub. On October 17, the Germans torpedoed the U.S. destroyer *Kearney* while it escorted a British **convoy**. On October 31, German subs sank the U.S. destroyer *Reuben James*. Each attack increased American rage against the Nazis and made it more likely Roosevelt could convince the country to go to war.

PEARL HARBOR

After Japan occupied **Indochina** in 1941, Roosevelt had cut off oil sales to Japan. He knew angering Japan was a risk. He began shifting U.S. bombers to the Philippines in case of an attack.

The attack came on December 7, 1941, when the Japanese bombed the U.S. Pacific Fleet at Pearl Harbor. Approximately twenty-five hundred Americans were killed. Eighteen warships were damaged or destroyed, including most of the fleet's battleships. Roosevelt had actually learned of the attack the day before, but was unable to send word in time. Roosevelt spoke to the American people the next day. He told them, "Yesterday, December 7, 1941—a date which will live in infamy—the United States of America was suddenly and deliberately attacked by naval and air forces of the Empire of Japan."

The attack enraged Americans. They had done their best to stay out of the war, and had been attacked anyway. Now

Bombing of Pearl Harbor

it was personal. The next day, December 8, Roosevelt asked Congress to declare war on Japan.

A few days later, on December 11, Germany and Italy officially declared war on the United States. Now Roosevelt was free to act. The Neutrality Act was no longer an issue. The Axis had declared war on the United States, and it would have to respond. Roosevelt met with Churchill in late December, and the United States joined the Allied forces.

ALLIED FRONT

From the start Roosevelt felt it was a better plan to deal with Germany first and then Japan. He met with Churchill; Josef Stalin; and China's generalissimo, Chiang Kai-shek.

Roosevelt addressing Congress on December 8, 1941

Eventually they all agreed on a strategy. The United States and Britain would attack Germany from the west. The Soviet Union would fight them from the east. China would face Japan in the Pacific with help from the United States and Britain. The United States would provide most of the weapons and supplies to the other countries. The coordinated attacks began in late 1942 and continued for the next few years. Germany blocked Allied advances at first, but battles in the Pacific were more successful. The Allies forced Japan back bit by bit after the Battle of Midway in June 1942.

By late 1943 the Allies were sure they could defeat the Axis. While they continued strategizing, talk turned to what would happen after the war. Roosevelt and Churchill met with Chiang in Cairo, Egypt, in November 1943. They met with Stalin in Tehran, Iran, a few days later. Roosevelt suggested a postwar organization of united nations. Stalin supported the idea at once.

In early 1945 Roosevelt traveled to Yalta, Ukraine, to meet with Stalin and Churchill again. Churchill had always distrusted Stalin and had warned other world leaders against the Soviet leader time and again. Churchill was convinced that the Soviets would not return their wartime conquests after the war had ended.

FINAL DAYS

In 1944 Roosevelt ran for a fourth term as president. His health had been poor for several years. The Democrats knew there was a chance he would not complete the term, and insisted that he drop Vice President Henry A. Wallace (who had replaced Garner in 1941). Roosevelt replaced him with Missouri senator Harry S. Truman. Together they won 53 percent of the popular vote, and thirty-six states.

Roosevelt continued to work hard after the Yalta Conference. He addressed Congress about the conference on March 1. He sent stern messages to Stalin about breaking their agreements on Poland and other matters. On March 29 Roosevelt traveled to Georgia. He was preparing for the founding conference of the United Nations.

On April 12 Roosevelt complained of a terrible head-ache. He collapsed and doctors confirmed that the president had just suffered a massive stroke. Roosevelt died the same day. His funeral was held at the White House on April 14. Roosevelt was buried in the Rose Garden of his Springwood estate in Hyde Park, New York. Germany surrendered three weeks later, on May 7, and the Allies accepted their surrender on May 8, or V-E Day (for Victory in Europe Day). President Harry Truman dedicated the day to Roosevelt's memory.

Franklin D. Roosevelt held the U.S. presidency longer

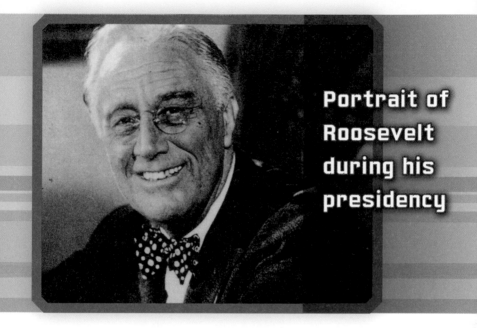

Portrait of Roosevelt during his presidency

than any other person in American history. He led the country out of the Great Depression and through World War II, and his reforms like Social Security and the Securities and Exchange Commission are still in place and benefiting us today.

HIROHITO

HIROHITO was the 124th emperor of Japan. He was in charge of the island nation throughout World War II. His decisions changed Japan forever.

EARLY LIFE

Michinomiya (or "Prince Michi") Hirohito was born in the Aoyama Palace in Tokyo, Japan, on April 29, 1901. His father, Crown Prince Yoshihito, was next in line for the throne. His mother, Princess Sadako, was the daughter of a prince herself.

Hirohito's grandfather Mutsuhito was still emperor when Hirohito was born. He was known after his death as the Meiji Emperor. He had been responsible for Japan's renewed trade and communication with the West after many years of isolation. Japan had closed its borders to foreigners in 1639. The country had been a military dictatorship then, and the emperors were mere figureheads. They had no real authority but still served as public figures. That time is known as the Edo period. It lasted for over two hundred years.

In 1853, however, U.S. Commodore Matthew Perry sailed his ships into the harbor at Edo. Perry demanded that Japan trade with the United States. He threatened to attack if the nation refused. Japan agreed and renewed relations with the West. Mutsuhito was a baby at the time. His reign as emperor marked Japan's transition from an isolated society to a modern world power. Hirohito had to live up to this legacy during his own reign.

Japanese royalty adopt different names at different stages of their lives. Hirohito was called Prince Michi when he was very young. Soon after his birth he was sent to a vice-admiral in the imperial navy. The vice-admiral's family raised Hirohito until November 1904. Then he returned to his parents' home at the imperial palace. Even then, however, Hirohito didn't spend a lot of time with his parents. He was supposed to focus on his duty to the nation, not on his family and friends.

Hirohito as a baby in 1901

TRAINING

In April 1908 young Hirohito started attending the Gakushuin, or Peers' School. This small and exclusive school was only for nobles and high-ranking families. Hirohito's class had a total of twelve boys, including Hirohito and two of his imperial cousins. The head of the school, General Nogi Maresuke, had been a hero of the Russo-Japanese War. Nogi took a special interest in Hirohito. He encouraged the young prince to study regularly. Nogi also taught

him the importance of hard
work, loyalty to the nation,
and the ability to ignore
hardship and pain.

Emperor Meiji died on July
30, 1912. Hirohito's father
became the Taisho Emperor
and Hirohito became the
crown prince and heir.
Hirohito got a new tutor,
Admiral Togo Heihachiro,
but he never felt as close
to Togo as he had to Nogi.

General Nogi
Maresuke

Hirohito was first introduced to **marine biology** around
this time. The young crown prince loved the subject at once.
Hirohito continued to study marine biology for the rest of
his life.

In 1921, Hirohito left Japan to take a six-month tour of
Europe. He was the first Japanese crown prince to travel
beyond his own country. Hirohito visited France, Italy,
Belgium, the Netherlands, and the United Kingdom. The
United Kingdom was by far his favorite, and he met with
the British king, George V, during his visit there. Hirohito
was fascinated by British culture, food, and clothing.

REGENCY

Hirohito's father's health began to fail that same year. The emperor was showing signs of mental illness as well. When Hirohito returned to Japan, he had to help his father rule the nation. Hirohito became regent on November 25, 1921. That meant he was now officially filling in for his father but his father was still technically in charge.

Hirohito's father, Emperor Yoshihito

A few weeks later, on December 13, Japan, the United States, Britain, and France signed the Four-Power Pact. The document confirmed that all four nations would respect the current state of the Pacific. None of them would try to seize property from any of the other nations. Japan and Britain also agreed to end the Anglo-Japanese Alliance. They had first signed the treaty on January 30, 1902. It had guaranteed that the nations would defend each other's interests in Korea and China. That alliance was partially responsible for Japan's joining World War I alongside Britain. They let the treaty collapse because it had been created to fend off Russia and Germany. By 1921 both nations were considered harmless.

A year later, another event shook Japan—literally. The Great Kanto earthquake struck Tokyo on September 1, 1923. More than 140,000 people were killed. Tokyo, the port city of Yokohama, and the areas of Chiba, Kanagawa, and Shizuoka all suffered severe damage.

On May 5, 1925, a different shock struck the nation. The General Election Law was passed that day. During Emperor Meiji's time, wealthy men gained the right to vote on government policies and activities. The General Election Law gave voting rights to every man twenty-five or older. This effectively weakened the emperor's control. He was still considered the supreme ruler, but now the government had millions of voters behind its decisions.

MARRIAGE AND HEIRS

One of a crown prince's first duties was to marry and produce a suitable heir. Hirohito became engaged to his distant cousin Princess Nagako, daughter of Prince Kuni Kuniyoshi, in early 1918. The couple married six years later, on January 26, 1924. They had seven children: Princess Shigeko in 1925, Princess Sachiko in 1927, Princess Kazuko in 1929, Princess Atsuko in 1931, Crown Prince Akihito in 1933, Prince Masahito in 1935, and Princess Takako in 1939. Princess Sachiko died when

Hirohito with his family

she was only six months old, but all of her brothers and sisters grew up, married, and had children of their own.

REIGN

Emperor Taisho died on December 25, 1926, and Hirohito assumed the throne. According to Japanese custom the Taisho era had now ended. Hirohito took a new name as emperor. He chose *Showa*, which means "Enlightened Peace." His subjects never referred to Hirohito by either name, however. They simply called him "His Majesty the Emperor," or "His Majesty." The official enthronement ceremonies were not held until November 1928, but they were strictly a formality.

When Hirohito took the throne, he learned he had less power than he had thought. The imperial army and navy had grown strong enough to veto government decisions. Both militaries often acted without orders. In 1927 they attacked Manchuria (now northeast China) and eventually wound up occupying part of that country. Hirohito had not authorized this attack and discovered he could not stop it, either.

In 1932 Japan's highest government official, Prime Minister Inukai Tsuyoshi, was murdered. He had overseen the military, and now the army and navy answered only to their own officers. A Korean revolutionary also attacked Hirohito that year by throwing a hand grenade at him.

Four years later, in 1936, several junior Japanese army officers led a revolt against high-ranking officials to take control of the government. They killed many leading politicians and occupied the center of Tokyo. Many high-ranking officers quietly supported the attempted **coup**. One of them, Prince Chichibu, was the emperor's own brother!

Hirohito was furious when he learned of the attempted revolt. He ordered that it be dealt with at once. His officers did not want to discipline their young counterparts, but Hirohito insisted. The rebellion was crushed a few days later, on February 29. The leaders of the revolt were tried immediately. They were found guilty, and some were sentenced to death. Hirohito had shown that he could take command when necessary.

AXIS OF EVIL

Japan invaded Manchuria fully in 1931. In 1937 Japan attacked China and began the Second Sino-Japanese War. Hirohito did not object to these conflicts but he did not suggest them, either. His staff and his prime minister had recommended both actions. Hirohito was most concerned about the Soviet Union; he worried that it might attack Japan from the north. To make matters worse, China and the Soviet Union were showing signs of possible alliance. This split China from its former alliance with Germany, however. Hirohito and his counselors saw a potential partnership there. Japan and Germany signed an Anti-Comintern Pact on November 25, 1936. The two nations agreed not to make treaties with the Soviet Union. They also pledged to consult and aid each other if the Soviet Union attacked either of them. That took some of the pressure off Japan. It also brought Japan and Germany closer together. A year later, in September 1937, Hirohito knew he had been right to partner with Germany because the Soviet Union formed the Sino-Soviet Nonaggression Pact with China. It began

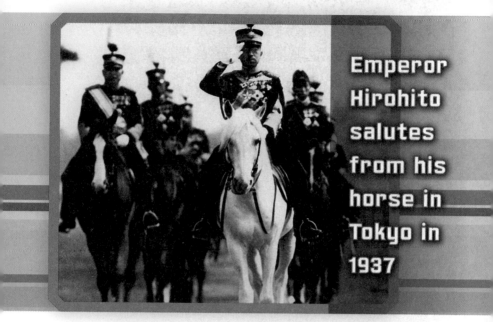

Emperor Hirohito salutes from his horse in Tokyo in 1937

sending China materials and weapons to defend against Japan's advances.

Hirohito authorized the use of torture against Chinese prisoners during the Second Sino-Japanese War. He also allowed his soldiers to use chemical weapons, including poison gas, against Chinese troops. The League of Nations had prohibited toxic gas but Hirohito authorized it anyway.

Japan continued to attack China throughout 1938. It took the Chinese city of Wuhan in October, but the Chinese government simply moved its capital to Chongqing instead.

In July 1938, Japan decided to go on the offensive against the Soviet Union. Japanese forces invaded the Soviet Union. They got as far as Lake Khasan before the Red Army blocked them. In May 1939 Japan tried again and attacked through Mongolia. The Soviet Union defeated them again, however. This second defeat showed Hirohito and his advisers that they could not win against the Soviet Union. China also continued to block their advances, so Japan turned its attention south. The United States and several European countries held islands in the Pacific. Japan concentrated

Japanese soldiers in
China in 1938

there instead, hoping to expand its influence and territory.

In July 1939, both the army minister and Hirohito's brother, Prince Chichibu, urged Hirohito to sign a treaty with Germany and Italy. Japan already had a loose alliance with Germany. Building on that arrangement would give Japan more freedom to expand its territory in the Pacific. Hirohito agreed, and Japan signed the Tripartite Pact with Germany and Italy on September 27, 1940. The agreement stated that Japan could conquer China and Southeast Asia without interference. In return Japan would not interfere with Germany's and Italy's plans for Europe. All three nations agreed to keep U.S. and British forces from taking control of the Pacific region.

Hirohito considered the plan carefully. He consulted with his prime minister, his chief of staff of the army, and his chief of staff of the navy. The two military commanders both agreed that now was the time to act. Finally Hirohito agreed. He signed the pact, and Japan became one of the Axis powers.

WAR EFFORTS

Japan's prime minister, Konoe Fumimaro, did not want the country to go to war. He became more and more concerned as he watched the nation's preparations. Finally he resigned his post. Konoe knew he couldn't stop Japan's march toward war, and he could not be involved any longer.

The army and navy suggested one of Hirohito's uncles, Prince Higashikuni, as a suitable replacement. But Hirohito did not want to put one of his family members in that position. If a member of the imperial family were prime minister, the entire family would seem responsible for the war and any consequences. Instead he appointed General Tojo Hideki to the post. Tojo agreed that they should proceed with the war effort, and Hirohito accepted his advice.

Japan was able to concentrate on its own region more effectively now that Germany and Italy were running interference in Europe and the Atlantic. Japanese forces continued to occupy central China and seized control of southern Indochina as well. In January 1941 Japan was fighting against Chinese nationalists. Stalin did not want to aid the nationalists in taking control, so he stopped helping China. Instead the Soviet Union and Japan signed the Soviet-Japanese Neutrality Pact in April 1941. They agreed to respect each other's territories and not attack each other. Japan had now neutralized one of its biggest threats.

Japan still hoped to claim the European colonies in Asia and take full control of the central Pacific. First, however, it needed to block or destroy the United States Pacific Fleet.

In mid-1941 Hirohito's chief of staff of the navy, Nagano Osami, brought him the suggestion to attack the U.S. fleet at Pearl Harbor. Hirohito quickly approved the idea, and they developed a plan. On December 1, Japan declared war on the United States and the United Kingdom. The Japanese attacked Pearl Harbor on December 7 and invaded Thailand and Malaysia the same day.

The attack on Pearl Harbor demolished the American fleet. Unfortunately, it also drew the United States into the war. Germany and Japan's other Axis partners responded by declaring war on the United States as well. Soon American troops were arriving to join the other Allied forces in Europe.

Fortunately for Japan, Franklin D. Roosevelt had decided to concentrate his efforts on Europe first. That meant Japan could act with only limited opposition. By the end of April 1942, Japan had conquered most of Burma, Malaya, Singapore, Rabaul, and the Dutch East Indies. It captured the Philippines in May 1942. It fought and easily defeated Allied ships in the South China Sea, the Java Sea, and the Indian Ocean.

The tide turned in early May 1942, however, when Japanese forces tried to capture Port Moresby in Australia. They hoped to sever the United States' communications and supply lines. The Allies intercepted the Japanese forces and prevented them from reaching the New Guinea port. Japan retaliated in early June by moving to seize the Midway Atoll (several small sandy islands in the North Pacific, roughly one-third of the way between Honolulu and Tokyo) so it could ambush the American carriers. The Americans had broken Japan's naval codes at the end of May, however. They knew exactly what the Japanese had planned. They turned the tables and soundly defeated the Japanese navy at the Battle of Midway.

Japan switched its focus back to Port Moresby. At the same time, the United States attacked Japanese positions on Guadalcanal (a tropical island in the southwestern Pacific) and the other southern Solomon Islands. The United States wanted to move in on the main Japanese base at Rabaul. Both nations began their attacks in July, but the Americans had more troops and pushed harder. By mid-September Japanese forces had retreated from Port Moresby. Australian and American troops drove them from the island after the Battle of Buna-Gona. By early 1943 Japan had lost the battle for Guadalcanal as well.

STEADY LOSSES

From spring of 1943 to spring of 1944, the Allies continued

to win ground against Japan. By March 1944 they had taken several islands from Japan and neutralized several major Japanese bases as well. Japan fought back, but was too busy attacking China to concentrate properly. Japan conquered several Chinese provinces by November 1944. By December 1944 Japanese troops in China and Indochina were able to join forces.

Japan was winning its battle against China, but things were going poorly in the Pacific. It had lost two major battles to the United States on Saipan Island and in the Philippine Sea in June 1944. Prime Minister Tojo had resigned in shame. The United States now had air bases near enough to launch bombers at Japan. In late October the Americans took the Filipino island of Leyte. They won another major battle at Leyte Gulf, landed on Luzon in January 1945, and conquered Manila in March. Japanese soldiers continued to defend the Philippine islands, but Japan's resources were spread thin.

In March 1945 American forces took Iwo Jima, part of the Japanese island chain. The Allies were now in Japan itself! They conquered Okinawa in June, and continued to close in on the capital in Tokyo.

Hirohito was heavily involved in the war effort. He received constant updates from the army and the navy. He followed their forces' progress carefully. Whenever possible, he encouraged his commanders to send in more men and launch stronger attacks. He appointed two prime ministers, Koiso Kuniaki and Suzuki Kantaro, after Tojo Hideki resigned, and encouraged them to continue the war effort. But Japan was losing ground steadily, and the Allies were drawing ever closer to Tokyo.

NAGASAKI AND HIROSHIMA

By early 1945 the situation looked grim. Hirohito met with several senior officials to discuss the war's progress and its eventual outcome. All except former prime minister Konoe recommended that Hirohito continue the war. They knew that Japan could not win, but hoped for one big victory to improve their bargaining position. Hirohito agreed.

In April the Soviet Union declared that it would not renew its neutrality agreement with Japan. That meant Japan could expect an attack at some point in the next few months. In May Germany surrendered to the Allies. In June the Privy Council decided to continue fighting, even though Japan now stood almost alone against the Allies.

By the middle of June, Hirohito's cabinet members had agreed to consider surrender. They decided to ask the Soviet Union to mediate for them. But first they had to prove they were still strong. The Allies would clearly invade the main islands of Japan soon. Hirohito's advisers felt they would be in a better position to bargain if they blocked that invasion first. Hirohito told his ministers to put together a concrete plan for ending the war, but they delayed.

On July 26, 1945, the United States, Great Britain, and China issued the Potsdam Declaration and called for Japan's unconditional surrender. Hirohito's advisers warned him to insist on several conditions before he agreed to surrender. Hirohito took their advice. He refused to obey the declaration.

Two weeks later, on August 6, 1945, the United States bombed the Japanese city of Hiroshima. At 8:15 A.M. the United States dropped an atomic bomb code-named "Little Boy." The nuclear detonation destroyed the city in an instant. It killed over forty thousand people that day and as many as one hundred thousand more over the next few months.

Three days later, at 11:02 A.M., the United States dropped a second atomic bomb, "Fat Man," on Nagasaki. Over forty thousand people died that first day. Another forty thousand or so died from the bomb's effects over the next four months.

That same day, the Soviet Union declared war on Japan.

Smoke rising from the bombing of Hiroshima in 1945

Hirohito immediately ordered his cabinet to draft an imperial document ending the war. He informed his family that he intended to surrender. On August 14 Hirohito notified the Allies that Japan accepted the Potsdam Declaration.

Hirohito decided to broadcast his surrender speech over the radio on August 15. He was the first Japanese emperor to speak on the radio. Most of the Japanese had never heard their emperor speak at all. In his speech Hirohito informed his people that he had ordered the government to accept the Allies' declaration.

HOPE FOR THE FUTURE

At the end of his speech, Hirohito told his people that he still hoped for a bright future:

"Let the entire nation continue as one family from generation to generation, ever firm in its faith of the imperishableness of its divine land, and mindful of its heavy burden of responsibilities, and the long road before it. Unite your total strength to be devoted to the construction for the future. Cultivate the ways of rectitude, nobility of spirit, and work with resolution so that you may enhance the innate glory of the Imperial State and keep pace with the progress of the world."

POSTWAR REIGN

Japan officially surrendered on September 2, 1945. It had been the last Axis nation left. World War II was officially over.

The world wondered what would happen to Japan now. People also wondered what would happen to the emperor himself. Many people felt Hirohito should stand trial for war crimes, along with other Axis leaders. Hirohito's family worried that the entire imperial line could be removed if he were found guilty. Some of them urged him to surrender the throne. They wanted one of his brothers to serve as regent for Crown Prince Akihito. That way Hirohito's dishonor would not stain his son.

Surrender of the Japanese on the USS *Missouri*

Fortunately for Hirohito, he had a surprising ally. General Douglas MacArthur, the commander of the U.S. forces in the Pacific, oversaw the United States' occupation of Japan. MacArthur knew it would be difficult to maintain order in Japan. Keeping Hirohito in place as the emperor would help calm the Japanese people. MacArthur made sure Hirohito and the rest of the imperial family were not put on trial. Instead, former prime minister Tojo Hideki was blamed for Japan's involvement in the war.

MacArthur and his staff soon took control of Japan. Their goal, however, was not merely to occupy the island

nation. They also wanted to
help it recover from the war.
They set up a food distri-
bution network to feed the
starving Japanese people.
The U.S. government and
several private relief organizations provided money and
aid. On September 27, 1945,
Hirohito and MacArthur met
for the first time. Hirohito
told MacArthur, "It was very
regrettable that circum-

MacArthur
and Hirohito
in 1945

stances led to war." If MacArthur held a grudge, he didn't
let it interfere with his plans. Instead he enlisted Hirohito's
support in making sure the occupation went smoothly.
Hirohito agreed. Soon he was traveling around the country, making public appearances and visiting factories and
schools. The Japanese emperor had always been a distant,
regal figure. This emperor who smiled and waved and
asked everyday people how they were doing was completely
new to Japan. The Japanese soon grew to love and admire
Hirohito more than ever.

Hirohito also traveled abroad. He went to the United

States and met with the new U.S. president, Gerald Ford. He traveled to Britain and met Queen Elizabeth II. Hirohito was now a public figure and a diplomat. His trips helped Japan build new bonds with other nations. Those bonds repaired Japan's reputation from the damage the war had caused.

Between trips and tours and speeches, Hirohito still found time for his own interests. He had loved marine biology since he was a boy. He had even built a laboratory in the imperial palace. He spent much of his time doing research, and published several papers and books on the subject. Marine biologists came to know and respect his contributions, but because the papers and books said they were "collected by His Majesty the Emperor of Japan" most of them never realized that Hirohito himself had written them.

END OF THE SHOWA ERA

The U.S. occupation of Japan ended in 1951. Japan was its own nation once more. Things had changed, however. The Diet, or parliament, had approved a new constitution in 1946. The document transferred most of the emperor's power to the people. An amendment the year before had given women the right to vote and strengthened the parliament and the cabinet. On April 10, 1946, Japan had

Hirohito with his son
Crown Prince Akihito

selected its first modern prime minister, Yoshida Shigeru. Hirohito was now little more than a figurehead. He was a symbol and a representative of the nation but not a real political leader.

Another change occurred after the war. Crown Prince Akihito fell in love with a commoner named Shoda Michiko.

President Reagan and the First Lady with Hirohito in Japan in 1983

In the old Japan, the emperor never would have allowed such a match. But this was the new Japan. Hirohito gave the couple his royal blessing, and they were married in 1959. The Japanese people were thrilled.

Hirohito's health began to fail in the mid-1980s. In 1987 he began experiencing problems with his digestion. Surgery revealed that he had duodenal cancer. Treatments seemed to help at first, but on September 18, 1988, Hirohito collapsed in his palace. He died on January 7, 1989.

Hirohito's death spelled the end of the Showa era. The

Japanese now refer to him only by his posthumous name, Showa Tenno or Emperor Showa.

Emperor Showa's funeral was held on February 24, 1989. Many world leaders attended the funeral, including U.S. President George H. W. Bush. Emperor Showa was buried in the imperial mausoleum in Hachioji, next to his father.

Hirohito was at least partially responsible for Japan's entering World War II, but he also helped guide his nation to a more democratic government and a new place in the world.

Hirohito in 1988

DWIGHT D. EISENHOWER

DWIGHT D. EISENHOWER was the thirty-fourth president of the United States. He is better known as one of the Allies' chief military commanders during World War II.

EARLY LIFE

David Dwight Eisenhower (who referred to himself as "Dwight David") was born in Denison, Texas, on October 14, 1890, but moved to a farmhouse in Abilene, Kansas, before his first birthday. Abilene is where Eisenhower grew up. His father, David, had studied as an engineer but dropped out to get married and had a hard time finding a decent job. Eisenhower's mother, Ida Stover, had met his father at Lane University in Lecompton, Kansas.

The Eisenhowers were a large family. Eisenhower was the third of seven boys. Sadly, his younger brother Paul died of **diphtheria** in 1895. The rest of the family moved to another house in Abilene in 1898. Eisenhower's uncle was able to get his father a job as a night foreman at the Belle Springs Creamery (dairy products were produced there).

Eisenhower (far left) in 1902 with his parents and siblings

EDUCATION

While Eisenhower was growing up, most people living out-side of big cities had only a few years of school. A lot of teen-agers worked on their families' farms or shops or had jobs of their own. Chores and work came before going to school.

The Eisenhowers believed education was important, however. They encouraged their boys to apply for college. The second oldest brother, Edgar, was the first to get into college. He got accepted to the University of Michigan. Eisenhower got a job at the Belle Springs Creamery, where his father worked, after he graduated high school in 1909. College was expensive so he worked to help Edgar pay for school. Eisenhower hoped to go to college himself one day, if he could afford it.

Eisenhower's friend Everett "Swede" Hazlett told him about the U.S. Naval Academy at Annapolis. If accepted, the academy would help him pay for school. Eisenhower applied to the naval academy and to the U.S. Military Academy at West Point as well. He passed the entrance exams

Eisenhower (center, front) on a camping trip in 1907

to both schools. But he was older than the naval academy's admission age.

Kansas senator Joseph L. Bristow took an interest in the boy's quest. He recommended Eisenhower to West Point. West Point accepted him, and Eisenhower left home to attend school. His parents were not happy about his going to a military academy. They didn't approve of violence, but they knew he would receive a first-rate education.

When Eisenhower enrolled he reversed the order of his first two names. His mother had always called him Dwight, so he made that his first name instead of his middle name.

Eisenhower enjoyed his time at West Point. He didn't make the varsity baseball team but he did join the football team. He was a promising running back and linebacker until a knee injury forced him to quit playing. Eisenhower stayed close to the sport, however. He served as the junior varsity football coach. His grades slid a bit after his football career ended, and he got in trouble several times for partying. But Eisenhower still managed to graduate West Point in 1915 in the top half of his class.

MILITARY STAFF

Eisenhower officially joined the U.S. Army as second lieutenant when he graduated from West Point. His first

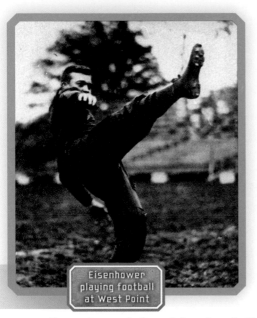
Eisenhower playing football at West Point

post was at Fort Sam Houston, in Texas. While there Eisenhower met a young woman named Mamie Geneva Doud. They married at the Douds' home in Denver, Colorado, on July 1, 1916.

A young military officer often got sent to new posts on short notice. The Eisenhowers moved to Georgia and then Maryland, Pennsylvania, New Jersey, then back to Georgia and Maryland. In 1917 their son Doud Dwight was born. Unfortunately, he died at the age of three from **scarlet fever**.

While in Maryland, Eisenhower's job was to train recruits for duty overseas. One of his responsibilities was training troops with the new tanks Britain had developed for World War I. Eisenhower hoped to go overseas and fight in the war himself, but he kept being denied. His superiors considered him too useful to send into combat. By the time they agreed the war had ended.

In 1922 Eisenhower became Brigadier General Fox Conner's executive officer in the Panama Canal Zone. He served there for two years and learned a great deal from Conner. The Eisenhowers' second son, John Sheldon Doud Eisenhower, was born in 1922 as well. John followed in his father's footsteps and eventually became a brigadier general in the U.S. Army, and then the U.S. ambassador to Belgium.

Eisenhower and his wife, Mamie Geneva Doud

Over the next nineteen years Eisenhower advanced through the ranks. He graduated first in his class from the elite Command and General Staff School in 1925. He served under General John J. Pershing at the American Battle Monuments Commission and was General Douglas MacArthur's aide and adviser in the Philippines. He was promoted to brigadier general in 1941 after he joined Lieutenant General Walter Krueger's staff at Fort Sam Houston. Yet Eisenhower had never commanded a unit in actual battle.

Eisenhower with MacArthur in the Philippines

ACTIVE COMMAND

After Japan attacked Pearl Harbor in 1941, army chief of staff General George C. Marshall summoned Eisenhower to Washington, D.C. He made Eisenhower part of the general staff in the War Plans Division. Marshall told him to come up with plans to defeat Germany and Japan. In 1942 Marshall promoted Eisenhower to major general.

In May 1942, Eisenhower was finally sent to Europe to report on the American forces' progress in Europe. In early June he returned, this time with the authority to reorganize the Allied forces with the British. In November he led troops into North Africa and by February 1943, his command had extended into Tunisia. The fighting in Tunisia let the Allies position their forces to hit key airfields and other targets in Italy.

Eisenhower led the invasion of Sicily. The invasion, labeled Operation Husky, began on July 9, with Allied landings along the Italian island's coastline the next day. By the end of July 10, the Allies had captured the port of Syracuse. The Allies also took control of the Pachino airfield on Cape Passero. Next they moved up the island and met German forces head-on. The Germans drove the Allies back in several places but lost ground as more American troops arrived. By August 17 all of the remaining German and Italian forces had left the island. Sicily was now in Allied hands. The Allies lost roughly 22,000 men in Operation Husky, including the wounded and those taken prisoner. The Axis lost 165,000 soldiers, however.

With Sicily under control, Eisenhower turned his attention to mainland Italy. This invasion, which consisted of operations Avalanche, Baytown, and Slapstick, began on September 3, 1943.

On September 8 Italy surrendered to the Allies. That did not change the Allies' plans. They knew they still had to defeat the Nazis. German troops controlled Italy's key defensive positions.

The German commanders knew they could not continue

to defend Italy without additional support. On September 16 the Germans broke off and turned back toward Salerno in order to withdraw. By early October the Allies had taken all of southern Italy. Most of the German forces had fled the country, though they had left some troops behind to defend their retreat. Italy was no longer a major concern in the war.

In December 1943, President Franklin D. Roosevelt appointed Eisenhower as supreme commander of the Allied Expeditionary Force. Eisenhower was responsible for planning the Allied assault on the coast of Normandy, France, in June 1944. The campaign, named Operation Overlord, freed western Europe and let the Allies launch an attack on Germany itself. The campaign began on June 6, which was code-named D-day. It involved an assault by 12,000 American and British planes, followed by an **amphibious** attack of almost 7,000 ships and tanks. Almost 160,000 troops crossed the English Channel on D-day. By the end of August the Allies had more than 3,000,000 troops spread across France.

Fighting along the beaches was heavy. Omaha Beach was the worst. The Americans who landed there faced the German 352nd Infantry Division. It was one of the finest of the German units and had the heaviest fortifications. The Americans took heavy casualties but eventually penetrated

EISENHOWER'S ORDER OF THE DAY

On the evening of June 6, 1944, just hours before D-day began and the Allies landed on Normandy, Eisenhower sent this letter around to all of the Allied troops. He had written the note himself. It took him several months to get it just right.

"Soldiers, Sailors and Airmen of the Allied Expeditionary Force!

"You are about to embark upon the Great Crusade, toward which we have striven these many months. The eyes of the world are upon you. The hopes and prayers of liberty-loving people everywhere march with you. In company with our brave Allies and brothers-in-arms on other Fronts, you will bring about the destruction of the German war machine, the elimination of Nazi tyranny over the oppressed peoples of Europe, and security for ourselves in a free world.

"Your task will not be an easy one. Your enemy is well trained, well equipped and battle-hardened. He will fight savagely.

"But this is the year 1944! Much has happened since the Nazi triumphs of 1940–41. The United Nations have inflicted upon the Germans great defeats, in open battle, man-to-man. Our air offensive has seriously reduced their strength in the air and their capacity to wage war on the ground. Our Home Fronts have given us an overwhelming superiority in weapons and munitions of war, and placed at our disposal great reserves of trained fighting men. The tide has turned! The free men of the world are marching together to Victory!

"I have full confidence in your courage, devotion to duty and skill in battle. We will accept nothing less than full victory!

"Good Luck! And let us beseech the blessing of Almighty God upon this great and noble undertaking.

"Dwight D. Eisenhower"

Eisenhower with Churchill in 1944

the German defenses. They took the beach three days later. British and Canadian forces managed to get through the defenses on Gold Beach and Juno Beach. The Allies then used temporary harbors, called Mulberry harbors, to unload more troops and material. They had hoped to capture all of the beaches the first day. It took three or four days instead because of strong German resistance.

On July 20 British troops marched on the city of Caen. The Germans committed all their tanks to the east to stop them. Eisenhower took that opportunity to send the U.S. troops through to the west. They pierced the German defenses and pushed through to Brittany. On August 8 American troops captured the German Seventh Army's headquarters at Le Mans. The Allies now controlled north-western France.

On August 9 the Allies moved to encircle the remaining German troops in France. By August 17 they had all but surrounded the Germans near the town of Falaise. German commanders requested permission to withdraw before they were completely cut off. Hitler refused. On August 21 the Allies closed the last gap in their defenses and trapped the Germans. Four days later the Allies freed Paris. By August 31 the last free German unit had retreated across the Seine.

Operation Overlord was a massive success. It signaled the start of the end of the war. The Allies were able to push German forces out of western Europe over the next few months. The Soviet Union attacked Poland and then pushed through to Germany itself. By February American and British troops had moved into western Germany. By March the Soviet army had advanced into eastern Germany. They captured the Reichstag, the German parliament building, on April 30, 1945. Hitler killed himself the same day. Germany surrendered on May 7.

Eisenhower had led the Allies to victory. He had still never been in combat himself, but he had won the respect of his commanders. He had also earned

the respect of leaders like Winston Churchill, Franklin D. Roosevelt, and even Josef Stalin. In April 1945 Stalin told the U.S. ambassador to the Soviet Union, "General Eisenhower is a very great man, not only because of his military accomplishments but because of his human, friendly, kind and frank nature."

AFTERMATH

Now the question was what to do with Germany. The Allies placed it under military law in May 1945. President Harry S. Truman appointed Eisenhower as military governor of the U.S. Occupation Zone. When Eisenhower learned of the

Eisenhower with President Roosevelt

Eisenhower, General Patton, and Truman in Berlin, Germany, in 1945

concentration camps, he ordered camera crews to document the camps for evidence in the upcoming war trials.

Eisenhower was also responsible for distributing food and supplies to German civilians. He recognized that most of the Germans were not responsible for the war. Many had only cooperated with the Nazis in order to survive.

In June 1945 Eisenhower returned home to Abilene. The town gave him a hero's welcome. He had become a hero to the entire Allied world, and Abilene was thrilled to have one of its own receive so much recognition.

NATO

In November 1945 Eisenhower returned to Washington, D.C. He replaced his former boss, General Marshall, as chief of staff of the army. A large part of Eisenhower's new job was demobilizing the millions of soldiers scattered across Europe and throughout the Pacific. He also counseled President Truman to maintain friendly relations with the Soviet Union. But Truman was too concerned about Stalin's plans and ordered Eisenhower to stop Stalin from expanding through Eastern Europe instead.

The president's refusal to listen frustrated Eisenhower. He couldn't accomplish much in Washington if his suggestions were ignored. In 1948 he left D.C. to become the president of Columbia University in New York. He was not entirely happy in his new job. It did, however, give him time to finish his memoirs. Doubleday published the book, entitled *Crusade in Europe*. It is Eisenhower's firsthand account of World War II, from his appointment by General Marshall to his actions as supreme Allied commander in northern Europe. The book was a tremendous success.

In December 1950 Eisenhower took leave from the

university. On April 4, 1949, the United States, the United Kingdom, France, Luxembourg, Belgium, the Netherlands, Canada, Portugal, Italy, Norway, Denmark, and Iceland had signed the North Atlantic Treaty. The treaty created the North Atlantic Treaty Organization, or NATO. It was a military alliance designed to defend its members against attack by any outside force. They offered Eisenhower the top position in the new organization. He accepted and became the supreme commander in charge of NATO forces in Europe. He spent the next eighteen months working with the NATO nations and their respective leaders and militaries to forge a unified defense against any threat.

Eisenhower was a popular figure after the war, and many people wanted him to run for public office. Both the Democrats and the Republicans had tried to convince him to run for president in 1948. He had refused. In 1952 the Republicans tried again. They began a "draft Eisenhower" movement to show him how much support he had from the American people. Eisenhower was impressed and moved. He was also concerned that the Korean War, begun in 1950, had not yet ended. And he worried about the leading Republican candidate, Senator Robert A. Taft. Taft wanted the United States to stop getting involved in conflicts overseas. He also wanted to stop Communism by attacking any he found in the United States. Eisenhower felt the country had to remain active on the world stage. He also felt the best way to handle Communism was diplomatically, and that the real problem was overseas rather than at home.

Finally Eisenhower decided he would accept the Republican nomination if he received it. He refused to campaign, however. But his friend Senator Henry Cabot Lodge, Jr., along with New Hampshire governor Sherman Adams and others, put Eisenhower's name on the New Hampshire primary ballot and campaigned on his behalf. When Eisenhower beat Taft 50 percent to 38 percent on March 11, 1952, Eisenhower admitted that the people had decided. He resigned as the head of NATO and retired from active service on May 31 and announced his candidacy for president on June 4.

Eisenhower promised to end the war in Korea. He also promised to maintain the country's involvement in NATO and to fight against Communism abroad and corruption at home. He and his running mate, Richard Nixon, won the election easily. Eisenhower took office on January 20, 1953.

PRESIDENCY

Eisenhower held office for two terms. He succeeded in ending the Korean War. In fact, the cease-fire was signed on July 27, 1953, only six months into his first term as president. He signed defense treaties with South Korea and the Republic of China. He also formed an anticommunist Southeast Asia Treaty Organization to block Communism from spreading further into Asia.

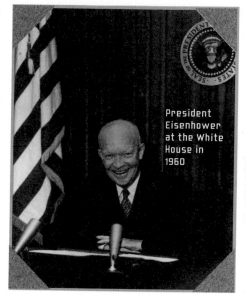

President Eisenhower at the White House in 1960

Spain was a Fascist nation at the time, controlled by Francisco Franco. But Eisenhower opened relations with them anyway. He formed a trade alliance and a military alliance through the Pact of Madrid. The new partnership helped guide Spain toward a time of prosperity and growth.

Eisenhower worked hard to establish a strong relationship with the Soviet Union, but that proved to be challenging. Eisenhower had dealt with Stalin during World War II. He felt the two of them had a mutual respect. But Stalin died in 1953 and Eisenhower did not know his successor, Nikita Khrushchev. The new Soviet premier seemed determined to expand the Soviet Union's influence throughout the world and had developed hydrogen bombs to compete with the United States'. Eisenhower tried to arrange **summits** with Khrushchev and other world leaders. The Soviets refused to attend or would not commit to anything specific during the conferences. In 1960 the Soviets shot down an American spy plane over their territory. Eisenhower claimed it was a weather research plane and had not been spying on them. The Soviets produced the pilot and the plane, which was clearly a spy plane. The United States had lied to the Soviet Union and to the world. The incident ended any chance of friendly relations between the two superpowers.

Eisenhower focused much of his attention on foreign affairs. He felt strongly that the United States should serve as the representative of democracy throughout the world. That meant they should encourage, support, and even protect other democratic nations. He did not concentrate as much on domestic affairs, but he did balance the budget. He also continued and even expanded many of Roosevelt's New Deal policies, including Social Security. Eisenhower managed to keep the national debt low, and allowed three small recessions to occur. During the recessions people spent less money and the country made less money. But that wasn't always a bad thing. Those three recessions helped balance out the inflation (rising prices) that had occurred during the war. He supported the Immigration and Naturalization Service's attempts to block illegal immigrants from crossing the Mexican border. Eisenhower was concerned that the immigrants would take jobs from American citizens.

In 1950 Wisconsin senator Joseph McCarthy announced that the State Department was employing several Communist Party members. The claim won him national attention. He continued to make accusations for the next few years and attacked many people across the country. He encouraged fear and hatred, and turned friends and business partners against one another. False accusations ruined many people's lives. Eisenhower despised McCarthy but refused to intervene directly, saying, "I will not get down in the gutter with that guy." He knew that acknowledging McCarthy would just give him more attention. Eisenhower did undermine McCarthy's authority, though. In 1954 the U.S. Senate's Subcommittee on Investigations began the Army-McCarthy hearings to investigate the senator's charges against civilian officials and the U.S. Army. McCarthy's behavior and claims cost him more and more support as the trials continued. On December 2, the committee voted to condemn McCarthy's conduct, 67 to 22. He left office a few years later.

In 1956 Eisenhower signed the Federal-Aid Highway Act, which created America's first interstate highways. It was the largest public works program in U.S. history. That same year he was reelected with an even wider margin than in his first campaign.

In 1957 Eisenhower sent federal troops to Little Rock, Arkansas, after the governor blocked a federal court order to **desegregate** the public schools there. Soldiers escorted the nine African American high school students to their school to make sure no one harmed them. Eisenhower then created a civil rights commission and a civil rights department in the Justice Department.

In September 1955 Eisenhower suffered a heart attack while on vacation in Denver. He returned to Washington in November, and by February 1956 his doctors said he had fully recovered. Eisenhower kept the press and the American public informed the whole time.

On May 10, 1956, Eisenhower was diagnosed with **Crohn's disease**. He had intestinal surgery in June. On November 25, 1957, he suffered a mild stroke. In 1958 he wrote a letter giving Vice President Richard Nixon control if he was incapacitated.

In 1958 Eisenhower signed the National Aeronautics and Space Act. That act created the National Aeronautics and Space Administration, or NASA. The agency handled the nation's space exploration and aeronautics research.

In 1959 Eisenhower admitted Alaska and Hawaii to the United States. They were the first states to join since New Mexico and Arizona in 1912.

QUIET YEARS

Franklin D. Roosevelt had won the presidency four times. After his death people worried about letting anyone hold power that long again. On March 24 1947, Congress proposed the Twenty-second Amendment to the Constitution. The amendment limited any president from holding office for more than two terms. Truman was exempt because he was in office when the amendment was ratified, on February 27, 1951. Eisenhower was the first president affected by the amendment. He couldn't run for a third term even if he wanted to.

Eisenhower didn't mind. In 1961 he said good-bye to the nation. In his farewell speech he warned that the United States needed to protect personal freedom and self-government. He also encouraged the country to maintain military strength but not to let that endanger the American way of life. Eisenhower concluded by praying for peace "in the goodness of time."

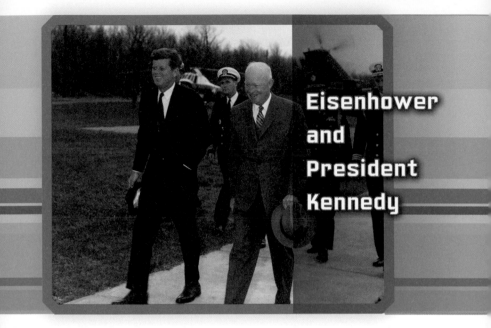

Eisenhower and President Kennedy

Thanks to the Former Presidents Act of 1958, when Eisenhower retired, he received a lifetime pension from the United States government. He and Mamie moved to their farm in Gettysburg, Pennsylvania. He spent his time raising livestock, gardening, reading, painting, writing his memoirs, and playing golf. In the evening he and Mamie sat on the porch, reading or playing cards or watching television. They traveled often, and spent winters at their home in Palm Desert, California. Eisenhower consulted with President John F. Kennedy, who had beaten Richard Nixon in the 1960 election. He also advised President Lyndon B. Johnson, who took over when Kennedy was assassinated in 1963.

Unfortunately, Eisenhower suffered a second heart attack in 1965. His health grew even worse in 1968. He spent time at Walter Reed Army Hospital in Washington, D.C., and died there of congestive heart failure on March 28, 1969. He was given a state funeral and then buried in Abilene next to the Eisenhower Presidential Library on April 2. His infant son Doud had been buried there in 1921. When Mamie died in 1979, she was buried alongside them both.

Despite never being in combat himself, Eisenhower led the Allies to victory in World War II. His calm approach to war and international relations helped the Allied forces work together smoothly and contributed to the peace and prosperity he brought the United States when he became president.

CONCLUSION

IT IS ALWAYS INTERESTING TO LEARN HOW DIFFERENT PEOPLE ARE connected and to see how those connections influenced them. Adolf Hitler started World War II, but he constantly worried about Winston Churchill and Josef Stalin and later about Franklin D. Roosevelt. His orders for Germany were partially based upon what those three men did with their countries. Churchill was one of the first to worry about Hitler's rise to power. But he was also worried about Stalin's ambitions. Churchill led Britain through the war but kept a close eye on both men. He worked closely with Roosevelt, however. Roosevelt was watching Hitler and Stalin as well. He was also worried about what Hirohito was doing with Japan. Hirohito's actions gave Roosevelt the excuse to bring the United States into the war. But Hirohito's biggest fear wasn't Roosevelt or Churchill. He was most afraid of Stalin. Half of Japan's actions were to make it strong enough to protect itself against the Soviet Union. Stalin didn't trust Hitler at all. He didn't trust

Churchill or Roosevelt, either. He signed a pact with Hitler to give himself time to position the Soviet Union. Then when Germany attacked, Stalin sided with Churchill and Roosevelt and helped them win the war. He'd hoped to go after Hirohito's Japan next but never got the chance. The war ended before he could act. Part of that was thanks to Eisenhower's quick thinking and careful planning. Eisenhower worked for Roosevelt and worked with Churchill and even Stalin to end the war. He controlled the Allied forces as they moved against Hitler and freed MacArthur to handle the Pacific forces against Hirohito. All of these men affected one another time and time again. Reading about the six of them one after another lets us see those relationships. It helps us see how they influenced one another, and the rest of the world. It gives us a better understanding of what caused World War II, and what happened during and after that massive conflict. The effects of those six men and that war are still with us today.

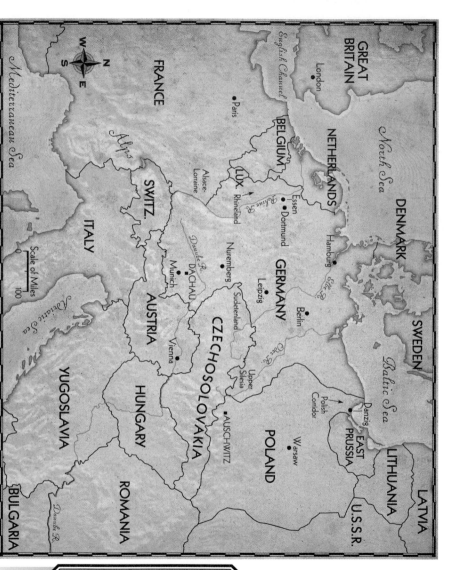

This map illustrates the borders of Europe in 1936, as established by the Treaty of Versailles.

Airlift: to bring in supplies by plane

Amphibious: working equally well on land and in the water

Apprentice: a person who is sent to learn a trade or profession from an experienced craftsperson

Austria-Hungary: a European power that included Austria, Hungary, Slovenia, Bohemia, and several other small countries

Axis: a partnership or alliance; in World War II, the alliance of Germany, Italy, and Japan

Boycott: to refuse to deal with another person, country, or organization to show disapproval

Cabinet: a group of senior officials who advise a leader

Coalition: a group that unites for a common goal

Conspiracy: a secret agreement to do something illegal or wrong

Convoy: a group traveling together for protection

Coup: an attempt by an individual or group to overthrow those in power and take control

Crohn's disease: a painful intestinal disease

Desegregate: to stop segregation, which separates people based on a single characteristic like race or religion

Diphtheria: a highly contagious disease that attacks the heart and nervous system

Economic sanction: one country's refusal to sell to or buy from another country because of something the other country has done

Exile: to send someone away and not allow that person to return

Guerilla: someone who is fighting those in power by using sabotage and stealth

House of Commons: a part of the British parliament consisting of members elected to their offices

Indochina: a region in Southeast Asia

Influenza: a respiratory disease that is particularly dangerous to young children

Manchuria: a region in Asia that is now northeast China

Marine biology: the study of ocean life

Memoir: an account based on personal memories or reflections

Mustard gas: a gas that creates a foul smoke that can choke and blind people; used as a weapon

Nationalist: someone who believes in a strong national government

NATO: the North Atlantic Treaty Organization, a military alliance designed to defend its members against attack by any outside force

Pact: an agreement

Parliament: a legislative body, usually with appointed representatives; the British Parliament consists of the House of Commons and the House of Lords

Patriot: someone who loves his or her country and works in support of its interests

Propaganda: information that is spread to help a cause or to do harm to an opposing cause

Protégé: someone who is helped and trained by someone influential or experienced.

Regime: the current forces controlling the ruling government

Revolutionary: overthrowing the established leaders for major change

Scarlet fever: a disease that causes a red rash and inflammation of the nose, throat, and mouth

Skilled labor: work that requires training

Socialist republic: a type of government in which everyone has equal rights and votes to elect leaders, and the government controls the economy

Soviet Union: the Union of Soviet Socialist Republics, a collection of fifteen Socialist republics united under a common leadership

Stroke: a medical condition caused by a blood vessel rupturing in the brain

Summit: a meeting of top officials, often world leaders

Treason: an attempt to overthrow those in power

Tripartite: having three parts

Tuberculosis: a bacterial disease that attacks the lungs

War correspondent: someone who reports on wars

BOOKS

Ambrose, Stephen E. *The Victors: Eisenhower and His Boys; The Men of World War II.* New York: Simon & Schuster, 1998.

Best, Geoffrey. *Churchill and War.* London: Hambledon Continuum, 2006.

Bix, Herbert P. *Hirohito and the Making of Modern Japan.* New York: Harper Perennial, 2001.

Brackman, Roman. *The Secret File of Joseph Stalin: A Hidden Life.* London: Frank Cass Publishers, 2001.

Bullock, Alan. *Hitler: A Study in Tyranny.* New York: Harper Perennial, 1991.

Churchill, Winston. *My Early Life: 1874–1904.* London: Scribner, 1996.

Dower, John W. *Embracing Defeat: Japan in the Wake of World War II.* New York: W. W. Norton, 1999.

Eisenhower, David. *Eisenhower at War 1943–1945.* New York: Random House, 1986.

Eisenhower, Dwight D. *Crusade in Europe.* Baltimore: Johns Hopkins University Press, 1997.

Fest, Joachim C. *Hitler.* New York: Mariner, 2002.

Henig, Ruth. *The Origins of the Second World War, 1933–1941.* New York: Routledge, 2005.

Hitler, Adolf. *Mein Kampf*, 1925.

Jenkins, Roy. *Churchill: A Biography.* New York: Plume, 2002.

Kershaw, Ian. *Hitler, 1889–1936: Hubris.* New York: Norton, 2000.

Leuchtenburg, William E. *Franklin D. Roosevelt and the New Deal, 1932–1940.* New York: Harper Perennial, 2009.

Medhurst, Martin J. *Dwight D. Eisenhower: Strategic Communicator.* Santa Barbara, CA: Greenwood Press, 1993.

Mosley, Leonard. *Hirohito, Emperor of Japan.* Upper Saddle River, NJ: Prentice Hall, 1996.

Nekrich, Aleksandr M. and Gregory L. Freeze. *Pariahs, Partners, Predators: German-Soviet Relations, 1922–1941.* Edited by Gregory L. Freeze. New York: Columbia University Press, 1997.

Overy, Richard. *The Dictators: Hitler's Germany and Stalin's Russia.* New York: W. W. Norton, 2006.

Roberts, Geoffrey. *Stalin's Wars: From World War to Cold War, 1939–1953.* New Haven, CT: Yale University Press, 2008.

Smith, Jean Edward. *FDR.* New York: Random House, 2008.

Ward, Geoffrey C. *A First-Class Temperament: The Emergence of Franklin Roosevelt.* New York: HarperCollins, 1992.

Wetzler, Peter Michael. *Hirohito and War: Imperial Tradition and Military Decision Making in Prewar Japan.* Honolulu: University of Hawaii Press, 1998.

WEBSITES

http://www.pbs.org/redfiles/bios/all_bio_joseph_stalin.htm

http://www.pbs.org/wgbh/amex/macarthur/peopleevents/pandeAMEX97.html

http://www.pbs.org/wgbh/amex/presidents/

http://www.spartacus.schoolnet.co.uk/

http://www.whitehouse.gov/about/presidents/

http://www.winstonchurchill.org/

INDEX